Get Paid for You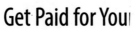

How to Maximize Profit From Your Airbnb Listing

GET PAID *For* YOUR PAD

JASPER RIBBERS *and* HUZEFA KAPADIA

Get Paid For Your Pad: How to Maximize Profit From Your Airbnb Listing

© 2014 Jasper Ribbers and Huzefa Kapadia.

Get involved today and take your Airbnb listing to the next level, visit: www.AirbnbAcademy.com

Published in San Francisco, California by Lifestyle Entrepreneurs Press. Lifestyle Entrepreneurs Press is a trademark of Lifestyle Entrepreneurs Academy Inc.

LIFESTYLE
ENTREPRENEURS
P R E S S

Cover Design by: Alan Hebel & Ian Koviak www.BookDesigners.com
Interior Design by: Stacey Grainger staceyderome@yahoo.com

Contents

Why Airbnb?
Size and growth
User friendly
Safety, trust, and verification
Sticking with one accommodations marketplace
Who is this book for?
How to use this book
Overview of "Get Paid For Your Pad"
The main message

Making your space "guest friendly"
Removing or storing personal items
Purchasing essential items that your guests will need
Ensuring your guests get a sound night of sleep
Bathrooms
Going the extra mile
Paying attention to presentation
Making your house smell nice
Investing in your house
Providing access to your house
Keyless entry
Lock and key
Managing your space
Monitoring your listing
Routine cleaning
Airbnb's pilot cleaning service
Check-ins
Doing it yourself

Discounts
  Negotiation position
  Substitutes
  Factors to consider when negotiating
  How well do the dates fit your calendar?
  What is the length of the stay?
  What types of guests are coming?
Extra charges
  Charging for cleaning
  Charging for additional guests
  Requesting a security deposit
Beyond Pricing

Communicating with your guests
  Pre-booking
  Inquiries
  Booking requests
  Inquiries to transact outside of Airbnb
  Post-booking
  Reaching out to guests during their stay
  Sending a post stay thank-you
Problems with your guests
  Broken or damaged items
  Unhappy guests
  Fixable problems
  Unfixable problems
  Handling guests who want to leave
  Issuing a refund
Feedback from guests
  Reviews
  Private feedback
  Asking guests for feedback
  Taking feedback seriously

Accepting bookings
Choosing your guests
Instant Book restrictions
Airbnb Host Guarantee
Most people are good people
Interacting with guests renting single rooms

The Airbnb review system
Overall Guest Satisfaction
Written reviews
Getting positive reviews
Your space must be clean
Everything must work
Writing a nice review for your guests
Asking for a review
Bad reviews
Taking them seriously
Leaving a reaction

Airbnb listing search
Search ranking factors
Verified factors
Inferred factors

What is next?
Thank you!

Prologue

I was done. Frustrated and fed up, disgruntled and exhausted, I knew that I had to leave my trading firm. For six long years I toiled away as an arbitrage trader: buying and selling stocks, futures, and currencies at a cutthroat pace. I had endured long hours, stressful work environments, and incessant verbal slings and arrows as I rapidly bought and sold goods to rein in profits for my firm.

Were the financial incentives impressive? Certainly. I was able to purchase a lovely two bedroom apartment in Amsterdam with one year's bonus check. But was the grind worth the reward? Did it make sense to be held financially captive to a laborious workweek and an unfulfilling profession? One day, those very questions suddenly had a clear and resounding answer: no and no. I had to leave. Right now. I could no longer sit idly by as months and years of my life slipped into oblivion. What good is a pile of money if the bulk of your life is confined to grueling tasks in a stale workplace? So in 2010, I marched into my boss's office, set down my ID badge, and tendered my resignation. And that my friends, was my glorious birth cry into ultimate freedom.

University

I loved my time at university. I enjoyed my classes and relished each and every opportunity to engorge my mind with delectable bits of knowledge. I was especially enamored with economics. As I delved deeper and deeper into the subject matter, I recognized that it was a breeze to understand and moreover, utterly fascinating. I couldn't get enough of the material, and began reading well ahead of my educational level.

In the spring of 2004, I graduated with a master's degree in Econometrics. I was 26 years old, completely broke, and eager to begin a new life as a financial trader. After receiving an offer at one of the top trading firms in the Netherlands, I was absolutely ecstatic. I would no longer have to worry about money and my life was to be henceforth filled with champagne brunches, steak dinners, and glamorous trips across Europe and Asia. I couldn't wait for the cash to start flowing and my new life to begin.

Life as a trader

"What is wrong with you, you stupid pig!! I told you about 10 times what to do, and you still blew the trade! You are a complete moron. Sit down, shut up, and don't do anything else until I give you further instructions. Idiot!!"

I had never been yelled at so cruelly in my life, but my fellow traders assured me that such treatment was par for the course. I had always been the top of my class, the brightest of the brightest, yet suddenly I was being referred to as a "stupid pig." The traders would beat me down mercilessly every time I fumbled a trade or miscalculated a profit. The high-pressure trading environment was something I had never encountered before, and while it was wildly exciting, it was extraordinarily intimidating. Large sums of money were on the line everyday, and people were constantly being berated for minor mistakes. I saw countless traders in tears every week, some eventually succumbing to the frustration and walking out the doors for good.

But I was resolute to stay the course. I wasn't going to give up, not unless they physically forced me through those doors. I absorbed the countless insults, shrugged off the unpleasant work environment, and endured the difficult lifestyle with a smile on my face. And lo and behold, after three long years, things started to get better. I got reasonably comfortable at the office, and trading started feeling more natural as well. My mistakes were infrequent, my financial success was increasing, and my demeanor was calm and stable.

Now, it's not as though trading became fun; it simply became bearable. The money, however, *was* a great deal of fun. It provided me with the freedom and flexibility to party at all of the best nightclubs, eat at the nicest restaurants, and travel the world at my leisure. Life was pretty awesome, and I wanted to take advantage of every pleasure available.

But in 2009, after working for nearly five years as a trader, something had shifted internally. I felt empty. Sure, I was being compensated well and my life was full of exciting trips, but my day to day was still a drag. I was bored and unhappy at the office, and I couldn't wait to get home. It just seemed like a perverse way to live life. So after a bit of contemplation, I shared my internal unrest with my boss. I explained that I wanted a change, but I didn't know precisely what to do. He thought about it for a few days and came back with an offer. "How about you take a position with our Chicago office?" he asked. I was intrigued. Although my day to day would remain relatively unchanged, it would give me an excellent chance to explore the U.S. So after I mulled over the opportunity for a few days, I accepted the offer and moved to Chicago.

Life in the U.S.

Chicago is a dense jungle of steel and concrete, laden with immaculate skyscrapers and high-flying condos as far as the eye can see. The entire downtown runs alongside Lake Michigan, a massive body of dark blue water that looks like the Pacific Ocean. Strewn along the waterfront are collections of beaches that are filled with bustling locals during the summer. Suffice it to say, I was absolutely in love with the vibe and the charm of the city.

My work life in Chicago was roughly equivalent to what it had been in Amsterdam, but I was so preoccupied with my new surroundings that I didn't let my job bring me down. I was on a constant mission to explore my neighborhood and meet new people. I even decided to treat myself with the purchase of a brand new Aston Martin sports car. Whizzing down Lakeshore Drive in a sexy convertible was a dream in and of itself. For a while, life seemed pretty sweet.

Internal turmoil returns

Every day I would: fire up my fancy cappuccino machine, fry up some eggs and sausage, devour a quick meal, shower, slip on my business casual garb, and head to the office. I would work all day, hustle back to my apartment, and enjoy the evening hours with my friends. It was a nice and easy life, one that many of my Dutch buddies envied.

But something was off. It had been nearly eight months since I had left Amsterdam, and as the awe and magic of Chicago had started to wane, I realized I was back at square one. I was still unhappy with my career. And a career, after all, is a central part of life. 10 hours a day, 5 days a week, and 50 weeks per year could not be devoted to a mind-numbing, soul-crushing profession. At least not in my vision of a perfect life.

So what was I to do? Should I quit? And if so, what would I do next? I spent several weeks thinking about my life and my aspirations. I struggled with all of the questions one might ask with regards to a life long pursuit, and finally came to an astonishingly clear conclusion: I wanted to travel. Yes, I know what you're thinking … that's not a career, right? I thought the same thing too, but I didn't care. I knew how I wanted to spend my life. I sincerely believed that everything would click into place once I began living my dream.

After a lengthy period of contemplation, I finally realized what I had to do. I needed to let everything go. I had to take the leap. If I didn't do it now, I would regret it forever.

So once again, I marched into my boss's office to deliver some bad news. But this time my resolve had shifted. I wasn't interested in conveying my woes and confusion. I didn't want any compromises or new opportunities. Instead, I was committed to leaving. I said the following: "Thank you for the wonderful chance to live in Chicago, but after a great deal of thought, I have realized that I can no longer work here." Sensing my determination, my boss barely protested, simply asking if there was anything he could do to change my mind. I said that my decision was made and although I had learned a tremendous amount at the firm, it was time for me to leave. He accepted my resignation, sent out a firm wide email notifying the staff of my departure, and let me go on my way.

I bolted back to my apartment with an electrified spirit. My body was surging with adrenaline, floating atop a euphoric cloud of excitement and anticipation. As I neared a busy intersection near my home, I paused. I watched the corporate worker bees scurrying home from their offices in a chaotic frenzy. It was a dance that I had done too many times. I took a deep breath, closed my eyes, and released any lingering tension in my body with a long exhale. I was no longer a member of the corporate tribe. What a lovely realization.

Now that I had once and for all cut the umbilical cord from my trading firm, it was time to set my master plan in motion. I arranged to have my belongings placed in storage, found a garage unit to house my car, and sold off whatever possessions I thought were no longer necessary. I was engineering a brand new existence, one that cast off the shackles of immovable baggage. I was determined to be lean, light, and mobile. I was going to be a free spirit.

Brazil and beyond

In the winter of 2010, I booked a one-way ticket to Brazil, packed my two remaining suitcases, and ventured into unchartered territory. I didn't know what I would do for money or where I would end up in the world; I simply recognized that I was taking the first step of an epic journey.

The next few months in Brazil were magical. I spent my days surfing and bouncing around the beautiful city of Florianopolis, meeting loads of locals and travelers everywhere I went. I was already fluent in Spanish, French, English, and Dutch, but Portuguese was a language I had never been exposed to. Since I felt such an attraction to Brazilian life and culture, I decided to study Portuguese. In two short months, I had achieved a solid fluency level allowing me to make even more friends in the region.

I felt so free and at ease! My life had morphed into a Peter Pan like fairy tale. I was no longer biding my time and gritting my teeth to make it through a treacherous and boring workday.

Instead, each moment was memorable and lovely. The idea of sitting behind a desk and working for a company seemed so distant and unappealing. I couldn't fathom ever going back to that life. Never again.

But I had one minor issue I had yet to resolve: money. Sure, I had some funds in the bank, but they wouldn't last forever. I needed to develop a stream of capital in order to finance my newfound lifestyle. Granted, I was living quite a humble life, staying in relatively cheap accommodations and eating inexpensive meals; but all play and no pay would eventually take a toll on my bank account.

At that point in time, I only had one revenue stream: the rent I earned from my apartment in Amsterdam. It made me a little cash, but not nearly enough to survive. So began my financial quest. I pondered a number of potential options such as: (1) starting various Internet related businesses, (2) buying and selling used automobiles in South America, and (3) diving head first into online poker. But all of those options turned out to be dead ends.

My research finally led me to a new method of monetizing property. Instead of renting out a home using a standard fixed-term lease, owners were now renting out small chunks of time just like a hotel. To make all of this possible, they were utilizing a new and revolutionary site called Airbnb, an amazing online marketplace for short-stay rentals. It sounded interesting, but the risks seemed way too high. How could I trust a complete stranger in my home, not to mention a stream of strangers over several years? Plus, I was already earning a solid cash flow from a straight fixed-term rental. How could I be certain that the short-stay market would be more profitable? But as I dug deeper, I realized that I could substantially magnify my annual income for very little additional risk.

I read everything I could about the short-stay business, and began setting up the necessary logistics. After a few months, I was making enough money to fund my travels. I was no longer eating into my hard earned savings; instead, I was staying afloat atop a sturdy raft of short-stay customers. And just like that, I had achieved absolute financial freedom! This was the lynchpin of my quest. This was the final answer I had been searching for. I could now spread my wings and glide effortlessly across the sky without a care in the world.

Still wondering how everything works out financially? Think of it like this: I'm roaming the streets of Bangkok with a few of my buddies, stopping on the street to grab some fresh made chicken pad thai and a Singha beer. As I take the first sip of my perfectly brewed beverage, my phone begins to vibrate. It's a notification from Airbnb. Someone has booked my apartment for the next 5 days at $200 a night! This is great news because I've now hit my average monthly target of 80% booking. This means that I have 24 nights booked, netting me a positive cash flow of approximately $4,000 (with costs factored in). After removing $70/per night to stay at the reasonably priced Aloft hotel (-$2,100), $30/per day for food (-$900), I still have $1,000 left over. That's plenty of cash to indulge my fancies and book my next plane ticket to a new and exotic location.

Today, my life is a dream. I spend several weeks in an amazing city, chronicle my experiences on my travel blog, and then pack up my belongings to enjoy another adventure elsewhere. I have been lucky enough to explore the Americas, Asia, Europe, and Australia. When I'm tired, I sleep; when I'm hungry, I eat; and when I feel like partying, I hit the bars of whatever city I'm currently residing in. I've met so many incredible and interesting people along the way. I simply can't get enough of life.

Many of my friends look at me in awe, wishing that they could have the wonderful and carefree existence that I enjoy. You know what I tell them? You can. The key catalyst in this voyage has been Airbnb. It bridged the gap from my former life as a trader to my current life as a world traveler. If it were not for this wondrous invention, I would likely have been forced back into a corporate straight jacket a year or two ago. But now I have security. I have a consistent revenue stream that allows me to remain in this fairytale like existence. In short, I am Peter Pan. The world is my Never Never Land, Airbnb is my pixie dust, and my entire life is my happy thoughts. Onwards and upwards to the next adventure.

INTRODUCTION

Getting Paid for Your Pad

*"Making money is a hobby
that will complement any other
hobbies you have, beautifully"*

- Scott Alexander, Author

As the world continues to transition into a highly global economy, folks are increasingly yearning for enriching travel experiences and cultural immersions. People are more curious than ever about the world at large and the vast strata of nations and cities. But as the enthusiasm for international travel has grown, there has been a simultaneous tightening of pockets. Translation: people want to travel on the cheap. This is quite a conundrum, isn't it? With exorbitantly high airline prices, expensive intra-city transportation, and costly big city restaurants, bargain traveling can be as elusive as the fantastical Lochness monster.

Of all the travel related money sucking goblins, the biggest beasts are luxury hotels. Don't get me wrong, I love a nice hotel. But while my senses are titillated by the extravagance and comfort, my wallet is met with a cold sucker punch to the gut.

Let's imagine "Joe the Traveler," a native of New York, wants to go to Paris for a week. Joe the Traveler is a planner. Accordingly, he starts searching for airline tickets well in advance of his trip and finds a reasonable deal: $750 for a round trip fare. He then sets aside $500 in cash for restaurants, since he will have to eat out for every meal. And he adds another $400 for alcohol and other miscellaneous charges. Grand total for a week amidst Parisians and croissants = $1,650. Not too bad for a seven day jaunt in Paris, right? Oops, he almost forgot... he still needs to book a hotel. Joe the Traveler loves a nice hotel, but Paris prices are pretty steep. According to his research, he's looking at spending upwards of $300 per night for a decent four-star hotel. That's $2,100 for the week! There is always the hostel option, but Joe dislikes those types of accommodations. He feels that while on vacation, he wants to be comfortable and a bit pampered. Even if he drops down to a three-star hotel, he's still looking at shoveling out $150 per night; a whopping $1,050 in total. What seemed like a lovely idea for a Parisian getaway has turned into an unseemly and grotesque expense.

But hope springs eternal. As the global marketplace continues to grow and adapt to the changing needs of society, a wonderful cost cutting mechanism has emerged from right beneath Joe's nose: short-stay rentals. Short-stay rentals (also called short-term rentals) are private homes that are subleased by owners directly to consumers. Instead of a homeowner offering a typical long-term lease (like six months or a year), an owner can lease out his domicile for a few days or weeks, similar to a hotel or hostel. Because these units are coming direct from owners and do not require the same maintenance and upkeep costs (such as employing an extensive management staff and housing expensive facilities such as restaurants), travelers can nab a terrific accommodation for a fraction of the price. Moreover, they have access to an actual home and all of the accompanying amenities. This means that tourists can: (1) save on the overall rental and (2) save on food costs by cooking their own meals. By booking a short-stay rental instead of a hotel, Joe the Traveler can now rent a private bedroom and bathroom in a luxurious condo in Paris for $75 per night, simultaneously cutting his food costs to $250 for the whole week (assuming he chooses to eat out a few times). That's $775 versus $2,600... a savings of almost $2,000!

From the consumer's standpoint, the short-stay rental is a marvelous bargain. A tremendous amount of cash can be saved without sacrificing comfort. But what about the other side of the transaction? Is it worth the hassle for homeowners to take on short-term guests?

Are you ready for the beautiful part? This is the beautiful part: short-stay rentals provide the ultimate middle ground for both parties involved. That's right, it is a win-win scenario. Not only do tourists save a solid chunk of change, but owners manage to rake in significantly more cash per annum than with standard fixed-term leases. And by significant, I mean 2x to 3x. I repeat, *2x to 3x*! Don't believe me? When I switched from offering a standard one-year lease to relying solely on short-stay rentals, my annual rental income went from a paltry $26,000 per annum to nearly $60,000! Moreover, providing short-stay rentals is extremely simple and convenient once the basic logistics are ironed out.

But there is one key problem: finding tourists to rent your place continuously throughout the year is difficult. Correction: it *used to be* difficult. With the emergence of an immaculately designed global marketplace for guests and owners alike, short-stay rentals are now easier than ever to arrange. What is this wondrous tool I speak of? It is the one and only *Airbnb*.

Airbnb was founded in 2007 by innovators Brian Chesky and Joe Gebbia. The product was first called "AirBed & Breakfast," and its initial purpose was to simply provide attendees of the annual Industrial Design Conference cost-effective short-term living quarters. The target market at the time was people who were unable to pay the hefty hotel prices in San Francisco. The goal was to offer a bare minimum bed and breakfast experience complete with a comfy airbed and a home cooked meal first thing in the morning.

It was a simple yet innovative concept in an industry that was hungry for change. From this basic prototype grew the awesome international marketplace we know today. The founders eventually changed the name from "AirBed & Breakfast" to "Airbnb" and expanded the scope of rentals to include: entire homes and apartments, private rooms, castles, boats, manors, tree houses, tipis, igloos, private islands, and other properties. Airbnb has drastically altered the travel sphere for the better, and has made the impossible possible for many wannabe travel buffs.

Why Airbnb?

Today, the accommodations market is massive. There are a plethora of websites and online tools that help travelers slice and dice hefty lodging costs into bite size morsels. For starters, there are sites like VRBO (Vacation Rentals by Owner), HomeAway, Couchsurfing, Roomorama, 9Flats, Wimdu, and HotelTonight just to name a few. These are all excellent websites with a variety of lodging options and terrific track records. But when it comes to product lines, there is always one that shines a little brighter than the rest. There is always one captain of quality that consistently provides the best level of service, the top products, and the highest level of overall value.

At the helm of this burgeoning industry, the so-called Neo of the accommodations matrix, is Airbnb. It is the most innovative and far-reaching company in the short-stay rental niche. Guests and owners alike choose to use Airbnb above all else because of its reliability and ultimate dedication to customer service. Personally, I have tried several competitor sites for my home in Amsterdam, and after a lengthy trial and error period, I have stalwartly decided that Airbnb reigns supreme for the following reasons.

Size and growth

Airbnb is a massive network of owners and guests that only seems to be growing bigger. As of 2014, Airbnb has hosted over 17 million guests at more than 800,000 properties across 190 countries and 34,000 cities. There were in excess of 6 million guest stays in 2013 alone, more than double the total in 2012. Of these 6 million stays, only 1/3 were within the United States. The remainder were spread across the globe, further supporting the fact that Airbnb has a substantial international presence that is only getting stronger.

The strident success of the company is garnering a lot of attention amongst financial investors in Silicon Valley. Co-founder and CTO Nate Blecharczyk has confirmed that Airbnb raised over $200 million in 2012 with the help of Founders Fund, a San Francisco based venture capital investment firm. More recently, Airbnb raised an additional $500 million in April of 2104. Even more impressive than a VC's vote of confidence is Airbnb's staggering valuation of $10 billion.

When you compare these figures to the competition, Airbnb comes out as an exponentially more successful and farther-reaching company. Wimdu, one of Airbnb's largest competitors, has only 300,000 properties worldwide. Roomarama, another major player in the accommodations space, has about 120,000 properties. Although these competitors have managed to develop strong reputations in the peer-to-peer rental industry, Airbnb remains the undisputed front-runner. Moreover, they have their sights set high, aiming for an eventual $1 billion annual revenue stream at 100 million stays per year.

User friendly

The Airbnb website is a breeze to use for both hosts and travelers. Sticking with a simplistic design and a natural feel, first time users are able to flip through the pages and find an appropriate lodging option within a few minutes. The landing page for the site greets users with a self-explanatory search box.

Once a user enters a **1** City, **2** Arrival and departure dates, and **3** Number of occupants, the search function launches into action and populates relevant listings according to location, price, and rating. The search results can then be refined based on a particular user's preferences.

Once a user has perused the listings and made a selection, all that is left to do is click the "Request to Book" button. A notification is sent to the host, and once he provides his approval, the short-term rental is confirmed and arranged.

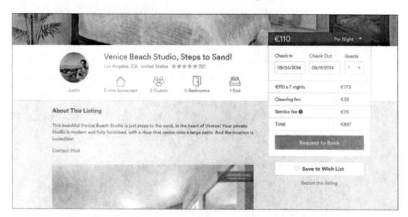

From the standpoint of the host, the process is streamlined and easy to use as well. When a traveler is interested in a particular property, he sends an inquiry message to the property owner.

Based on availability, reviews, and whatever other criteria a host chooses to examine, the traveler will either be accepted or denied a booking. As each acceptance is made, the host's calendar of available dates is automatically updated.

Safety, trust, and verification

Safety is the single biggest concern potential hosts have when renting out their house. Many folks feel that inviting unknown strangers into their homes is an unpredictable liability. Despite the upside of making a decent stream of supplemental income, hosts worry themselves sick over the following list of questions and concerns:

- What if a guest steals my belongings?
- What if my home is damaged?
- What if my guest is highly unsanitary?
- How can I be sure that my guest will not harm me?
- How can I be certain that my guest will not bring an unwanted pet or animal into my home?

These are all reasonable concerns when dealing with complete strangers. But don't fret just yet. Airbnb has recognized these potential perils and implemented a number of highly effective protective measures.

1. **The Airbnb Host Guarantee** – Airbnb has guaranteed all hosts up to $1,000,000 in damages and losses on each and every rental. It is complimentary protection and the policy is backed by Lloyd's of London. Although the coverage is fairly broad, the following items fall outside the scope of the coverage:

    -   Normal wear and tear
    -   Cash and securities
    -   Collectibles
    -   Rare artwork
    -   Jewelry
    -   Pets
    -   Personal liability

    For more information on how to file a claim, you can check out the Airbnb Host Guarantee FAQ page.

2. **Profiles and reviews of potential guests** – Airbnb is a short-term rental social network. Guests and hosts alike are encouraged to create profile pages with pictures, videos, personal information, reviews, and references. Hosts can take advantage of the wealth of personal information available before accepting a guest. Airbnb encourages users to look at reviews, read personal references, examine photos and videos, and make sure that the guest feels like a good fit. At the end of the day, the best safety measure is a bit of due diligence.

3. **Security deposits** – If a host wants to implement a financial failsafe, he is free to require a security deposit. The amount of the deposit can be anywhere from $100 to $5,000. In order to use this protective measure, the security deposit must be in place before the reservation is made. A host is not allowed to

retroactively apply a security deposit to an established rental agreement. If a problem does arise during the rental period and damage has occurred, a host has 48 hours to report the issue. If a report is not made within the allotted time, the host must release the security deposit.

4. **Messaging capabilities between hosts and potential guests –** When a potential guest wants to reserve a home, he will usually shoot the host a personal message. Hosts then have the opportunity to communicate with the potential client and ask why he is in town, what he does for a living, how many people he is traveling with, etc. This is a terrific opportunity to gather a bit more intelligence before handing over the keys to the castle.

5. **Reservation requirements –** Hosts can require that all guests have Verified ID. This will ensure that they have been reviewed and approved by the Airbnb staff.

6. **Guest guidelines –** Airbnb provides hosts with two awesome ways to help keep their guests in line: House Rules and a House Manual. The House Rules provide hosts with the opportunity to outline precisely what is acceptable and what is not permitted during the visit. Potential guests can see these rules before a reservation is even requested. The House Manual is private information that is shared with guests only after the reservation is confirmed. It can provide tidbits such as the WiFi password, operation instructions for the dishwasher, and the location of the nearest café.

The bottom line is that hosts have a number of excellent tools at their disposal to learn about guests. If at the end of the inquiry, a host feels unsure about a potential guest, he is always free to reject an application and move on to another request.

Sticking with one accommodations marketplace

There are multiple accommodations websites where you can list your space for short-term stays. When I began renting out my flat, it seemed logical to utilize all available avenues. I presumed that if I only listed my space on Airbnb, I would miss out on a number of potential guests that were using other sites.

Since Wimdu had the next largest market share in my region, I created a second profile on the Wimdu platform. After a few months of double dipping my flat, I realized that I wasn't getting nearly as many bookings through Wimdu as with Airbnb. But since I was getting some traction on Wimdu, I decided to keep both of my profiles. Two profiles are better than one, right?

But then I started thinking about my rental strategy a little more deeply. I did some research on the various accommodations websites and scoured whatever travel message boards I could find. After much contemplation and consideration, I finally decided to delete my Wimdu account and focus solely on Airbnb. Why? Here's why:

- **User reviews, ratings, and bookings are the key to success** – Spreading your listing across several sites can hamper your ability to boost your bookings on Airbnb. Say, for example, a traveler happens to use Wimdu before Airbnb. That means that once they locate your spot on Wimdu, your room will be booked through that website. No big deal, right? In the short-term maybe not, but this can have grave effects in the long run. If your ratings, reviews, and bookings are evenly dispersed amongst several listings on different platforms, you will fail to optimally boost your rank and reputation on any one website. This, in turn, will drastically impact your success in a negative way. This can be so detrimental because the algorithms that are used to pull up your listing from a region-based search are highly influenced by user feedback and overall booking numbers. As you climb the search ranks, your booking rate will increase exponentially, not linearly. This is similar to the distribution of clicks that webpages receive from Google search results. Page one results usually net 80 - 90% of the total clicks, while the countless pages thereafter are fighting for mere scraps. This means that placing your listing on multiple sites can potentially cost you: (1) a lot of bookings and (2) a great opportunity to raise your prices in tandem with higher demand.

- **Airbnb is an integral part of a short-stay rental search –** Since Airbnb is the biggest and most well known of the accommodations sites, it is usually the first choice of guests. If, however, a user chooses to glance at several sites in his quest for a rental space, there is a large likelihood that Airbnb will be amongst the list of websites utilized. Accordingly, even if you're not on other sites, most people will still come across your listing.

As with all strategies, there are of course exceptions. If, for example, your property is located in an area with very low demand, it could make sense to list your home on a few different sites. When competition is low, there is less of a need for a solid reputation because differentiation is not as necessary for success. By virtue of the low supply, your listing will invariably be high up on the search results.

Who is this book for?

This book has been written for two groups of people:

1. Current Airbnb hosts who want to improve their earnings

2. Property owners who are short-stay rental novices

For current hosts, I want to give you the keys to the kingdom. I aim to provide you with a comprehensive toolkit so that you will be empowered to get your listing firing on all cylinders. Your goal should be to become the best host possible. This will in turn mean that your search rank will be extremely high within your neighborhood, your price will be maximized, and your listing will attract the highest quality guests available.

For group number two, the short-stay rental novices, I seek to open your eyes to the endless possibilities. Many homeowners are highly reluctant to enter this business because of the seeming complexity of managing streams of visitors. Not only that, they are deterred by the apparent risk of hosting strangers. But as I've explained already, the risks are manageable. Hosts have complete control over what guests they take in, and accordingly, how much risk they take on. And sure, renting to a single person for an entire year might seem vastly simpler, but once the basic logistics are arranged, the process is not that time-intensive. Moreover, the financial benefits are more than worth the added effort. Doubling, or in some cases, tripling your net income over a fixed-term lease is certainly something to take heed of.

Although this book has been written specifically for Airbnb hosts, many of the concepts can be applied to other accommodations websites. Again, it is my view that the sole use of Airbnb will yield the best results in most cases, but if you are so inclined, feel free to apply these basic principles to any and every listing you choose to create.

How to use this book

This guide is an all-encompassing reference on how to optimize your Airbnb listing and maximize your rental income. It contains everything you need to know to ensure that you will draw in the maximum amount of money from your listing. Unlike other Airbnb books, *Get Paid For Your Pad* isn't meant to be a one-time read. You could certainly flip through it in a day, but the idea is have this book beside you while you create or tweak your listing. I suggest reading it in its entirety once, and then pulling it up periodically as you attempt to improve your particular listing.

This book covers every single aspect of hosting on Airbnb. Because I will dive into intricate details, the material might feel overwhelming at times. Accordingly, make sure to re-read each section while editing your listing. For example, when you find yourself sitting down to whip up an awesome guidebook, flip to the corresponding section and read through it as you work. *Get Paid For Your Pad* will serve as a map to help you navigate through the listing labyrinth.

Overview of "Get Paid For Your Pad"

Chapter one, **Preparing Your House**, covers everything you'll need to know to adequately prepare your house for your guests' arrival. It identifies items that should be removed, lists appliances that your guests might need, describes how to create comfortable sleeping arrangements, and explains how to provide access to your house.

Chapter two, **Creating A Killer Listing**, covers the ins and outs of drafting a killer Airbnb listing. I will delve into profiles, titles, descriptions, house rules, cancellation policies, and the minimum and maximum amount of nights you should accept.

Chapter three, **Pricing**, covers the complex and potentially confusing quest to find an optimal price point. I explain how to: (1) find a pricing strategy for a new listing, (2) adjust the pricing for an existing listing to match demand, and (3) negotiate with a bargain hunting guest.

Chapter four, **Your Guests**, is arguably the most important chapter of the book. How you communicate with and treat your guests will determine the longevity and success of your listing. I suggest that you study this chapter carefully and avoid being complacent with regards to customer service. The chapter covers a wide array of subjects, such as: (1) how and when to communicate with your guests, (2) what to do when a problem arises, and (3) how to get feedback.

Chapter five, **Reviews**, examines the Airbnb review protocol. Getting positive reviews is essential to increasing the number of inquiries and bookings that you will receive. I will explore: (1) the inner workings of Airbnb Guest Satisfaction ratings, (2) how to get positive reviews, and (3) how to handle bad reviews. Although bad reviews can definitely hurt, there is a way to minimize damage and potentially use them to your advantage.

The last chapter of the book, **Promoting Your Listing**, deals with how to advertise your space. Although there are several ways to promote your listing, the most important channel is of course the Airbnb Search Results. This section parses all of the details to secure a prominent position in the results. Reaching page one in the search ranks for your neighborhood or city will be essential for reeling in a hefty chunk of change.

I have peppered this book with a number of examples and templates that I use when managing my listing. These have been included so that you can use these references as a guiding hand when crafting your own profiles or guest communications.

The main message

This book aims to transform you into a super-amped ultra host. Why? Because the integral catalyst for augmenting your rental income is the quality of service you provide. In the short-stay rental business, customer service and overall quality reign supreme. This book is not about tricks or tactics, it is about: (1) creating an awesome product, (2) spreading the word about your amazing property, and (3) making your guests feel welcomed and comfortable. In short, the only recipe for success is being the best host you can be.

CHAPTER 1

Preparing Your House

"Before anything else, preparation is the key to success."

- Alexander Graham Bell,
Inventor and Scientist

Before you create your listing, you must ensure that your space is ready to receive guests. So what is the appropriate standard to follow? When contemplating this question, it's important to bear in mind that most guests envision a vacation to be nothing short of picturesque. Most folks are accustomed to a plush hotel lobby, friendly hotel staff, and an assortment of complimentary travel goodies.

No, you shouldn't begin construction on a spiraling staircase and a magnificently gaudy chandelier. I am not suggesting that you aim to recreate a hotel atmosphere verbatim. The goal here is to provide comfort, peace of mind, and the impression that your guest is being taken care of. You want to create a carefree vacation vibe where questions are answered, concerns are addressed, and needs are met and exceeded. You are now part and parcel of a vacation fantasy factory. Your job is to build the best experience possible to ensure that your lovely guests experience a magical holiday in your city.

Making your space "guest friendly"

Transforming your space from a private living area to a guest friendly unit can take some doing. There are a number of details to attend to; some are intuitive, others are not. Below is a step-by-step guide on how to prepare your apartment or house for all types of travelers.

Removing or storing personal items

First things first: remove personal items that are not useful for guests. There is no reason to have your personal belongings strewn about the apartment. You probably don't want your guests to try on your favorite pajamas, and they don't want to see your toothbrush and razor in the bathroom. Here is a quick list of items that you should try and store elsewhere:

- Clothes
- Personal toiletries (razors, toothbrushes, medications, etc.)
- Computers
- Shoes
- Jewelry
- Personal documents
- Personal photos

There are, of course, certain items that could be useful to your guests. I typically leave the following personal items:

- Books
- Movies
- Video games
- Magazines

And, in case you're wondering, I have never had a personal item stolen.

Purchasing essential items that your guests will need

Here's what you're shooting for: a home away from home. The central goal of a stellar host is to make the apartment feel familiar and comfortable. The best place I've ever rented on Airbnb was a duplex apartment on the island of Hvar in Croatia. A couple of my buddies and I rented out an awesome condo in the heart of the city. The location was incredible, and the host was very kind, but the amenities are what made it a truly memorable stay. We had a fully stocked kitchen with amazing appliances, an in-house laundry machine, a loaded linen closet, two TVs with satellite, and a collection of blockbuster movies. It was pretty awesome to say the least.

But why did it feel so special? It was the amazing little extras that made us feel at ease. It was the intrinsic familiarity that seemed to transcend international borders. As soon as I walked into the apartment, a wave of calm washed over me. I instantly felt comfortable. As a host, my goal is to engender that same feeling of familiarity for each and every one of my guests. After hosting nearly 100 groups at my place and heeding their requests and suggestions, I've assembled a comprehensive list of all the basics that make a space truly welcoming:

Bedroom supplies

- Extra blankets
- Extra pillows
- Towels
- Baby crib
- Extra air mattress
- Alarm clock

Bathroom supplies

- Paper towels
- Toilet paper
- Tissue
- Liquid soap and shampoo
- Bathroom hooks for hanging clothes and towels
- Hair dryer
- Disposable razors and shaving cream
- Toothpaste

Kitchen supplies

- Microwave
- Toaster/toaster oven
- Tea pot
- Salt
- Sugar
- Oil
- Coffee maker
- Salad mixer
- A high quality knife and cutting board
- Two pans and two pots
- At least four sets of basic utensils

Cleaning supplies

- Odor neutralizing spray (e.g. Febreze)
- Broom
- Vacuum
- All-surface spray cleaner

Even if you are only renting out a two-bedroom place, you might very well have four to five guests residing in your apartment at once. Accordingly, I suggest having sufficient linens and bedding material for multiple guests.

Ensuring your guests get a sound night of sleep

One of the most important components to providing a comfortable stay is making sure that your place is conducive to a good night's rest. Lumpy mattresses, annoying sounds or noises, or uncomfortable linens can be a sure fire way to a negative review. There are some really simple and inexpensive things that you can do to make sure your guests have a deep and relaxing slumber at your home:

- Install drapes and curtains that completely block out all outside light
- Fit your bed with a soft foam top
- Provide different blankets for warm/cold nights
- Leave an eye-mask and ear plugs by the bed
- Place a small fan in the bedroom

Bathrooms

Attention: your bathrooms must be immaculate! Remember, the standard you are competing against is a luxury hotel. When is the last time you checked into a five-star establishment and saw a single spec of dirt in the bathroom? Your toilet must be scrubbed to perfection, your sink must be free of all particulates, and your shower must not have an inkling of mildew. That is your base-line standard. For guests who are very clean themselves, having a moderately clean bathroom can ruin the entire stay. Bathrooms are very intimate spaces. People must feel secure and safe while using bathroom facilities.

Going the extra mile

If you implement the suggestions I've already listed, then you are on your way to a stellar review. But, if you want to strive for absolute excellence and true five-star caliber service, you will have to go the extra mile. If you're up for the challenge, here are a few supercharged suggestions:

- Provide a cell phone with a local sim-card
- Offer discount coupons to tourist attractions, restaurants, and bars
- Leave a collection of menus for nearby restaurants
- Give your guests access to bicycles
- Provide public transportation cards
- Offer an airport pick-up service

Paying attention to presentation

Top-notch service is not just about *what is available*; it's about *how it is presented*. You've seen the show Top Chef, right? While excellent ingredients and perfect seasonings are a must, what separates the wheat from the chaff is presentation. It's all about the arrangement of the items: the colors, the symmetry, and the overall artistic flair. Just like competitive cooking, presentation is key in the short-stay rental game as well.

Here are a few quick tips on how to make your place look as prim and proper as a lavish resort:

- Perfectly folded towels with a bottle of shampoo and a soap packet on top

- A mint or chocolate on the bed accompanied by a brief welcome note

- A six pack of beer in the fridge

- An assortment of apples and oranges in a decorative bowl on the kitchen table

Making your house smell nice

My favorite hotels in the world are the Shangri-La hotels. They have impeccable service, lush accommodations, and scrumptious food. But you know what I always remember? What always makes me feel at home as soon as I walk through those lovely revolving doors? It's the pleasant and familiar Shangri-La smell. As soon as I enter the hotel lobby, I am warmly welcomed by a fresh and crisp floral aroma. It feels so good.

🏃DO THIS NOW

Take a quick tour around your house. Go through each and every room and ask yourself: (1) what is missing and (2) what is not necessary. Take inventory, write a list, and get moving.

This is the atmosphere you want to create for your guests. You need to fill the air with an inviting aroma (without over-powering their nostrils). This will not only make your guests feel at ease, but it will reinforce the idea that your place is extraordinarily clean. I recommend using neutral smells from products with mass appeal. Some examples of terrific aromatic tools are as follows:

- Glade plug-ins
- Febreze Noticeables
- Hamilton Beach True Air
- Scented candles (in order of the most popular scents)
  - Chocolate
  - Fresh Laundry
  - Lavender
  - Lemon
  - Sandalwood
  - Apple
  - Rose
  - Coconut
  - Cookie
  - Vanilla

Investing in your house

When it comes to providing your guests with basic amenities, it should be astoundingly clear that this is a must. The basics are relatively low cost items that will be met with a high level of appreciation by your guests. Translation: it is a minimal investment for a truckload of glowing reviews.

But what about big-ticket items? Friends often ask me if they should purchase a $1,000 mattress or a $3,000 flat screen television. Sure these would be nice additions, but you must view all of your purchasing decisions as investment vehicles. When deciding whether or not to buy an expensive item, consider the incremental money you will be able to charge a guest.

Think about it this way: let's say you are considering buying a new mattress for your house. Your current bed is moderately comfortable and slightly worn down, and the one you have your eye on is phenomenally plush and costs $1,000. Should you buy it? Let's consider the numbers.

First off, how much do you think guests would be willing to pay for a substantially better mattress? One dollar more per day? Two? There is no direct answer to this question, so the best any host can do is implement logic and common sense. Let's assume that an expensive and comfortable bed could reasonably justify a price hike of at least $3 per night. Assuming your apartment is rented approximately 200 days per year, this new addition would yield $1,200 after two years... a net profit of $200. So you should buy the mattress, right? Not so fast, cowboy.

Before you call up your local mattress retailer, you need to consider opportunity cost. For example, could you hike the price an equivalent amount by springing for a top of the line $200 foam top? If so, you could earn a profit of $1,000 in two years! For your convenience, I have compiled a quick list of keystone items that will boost your value in a cost-effective manner.

- A reasonably priced LCD TV – $400-$500
- A very comfortable foam top mattress – $100-$200
- In unit laundry machine – $700-$900

A great way to determine how to optimally invest your money is by reviewing your guests' feedback. Look at both your reviews and private messages to see what suggestions have been raised. This is a highly valuable research mechanism at the disposal of every host. Take advantage of it.

Providing access to your house

Hotels are dependable. Even three-star establishments have reliable front desks with 24-hour service. That means that new guests can walk in at any time and have someone assist them with a check-in. It's a great feeling to know that someone will always be there at your beck and call. Moreover, if a key is misplaced, guests can simply ask for a replacement with minimal hassle.

How can you provide a similar level of service without building a front desk and hiring a staff? Simple.

Keyless entry

The newest fad for hosts across the globe is to install an electronic locking system. These technologically savvy options enable guests to simply enter a numeric code (or provide a finger print) to gain access to the unit. The code can be changed remotely as guests cycle in and out of your home. This option is particularly attractive to hosts who are frequently on the road. Guests can check into the home without any sort of a liaison (although we still recommend a personal greeting when possible).

Another benefit of these remote locking systems is that they can send notifications to hosts if the front door is left open for an extended period of time. Depending on the brand, arrays of customizable options are available regarding messaging and personalization. Finally, electronic locks simplify the entire experience by negating the need for multiple keys. Guests don't have to worry about losing a key or locking themselves out of the apartment.

For your convenience, I have assembled a short list of some terrific electronic lock products in the table on the next page.

Lock	Price	Details	Photo
ResortLock RL2000	$299	The RL2000 is a good option at a relatively high price. The lock has the capacity for 800 permanent user codes, and can be preprogrammed to open and lock at particular times of the day. It runs on 4AA batteries. The RL2000 usually requires a complete reinstallation of the lock.	
Lockitron	$179	The Lockitron lock fits on most existing cylindrical residential dead-bolt style locks. It integrates with any phone and delivers customizable messages. The lock can also be pro-grammed to open via text message.	
Schlage Camelot Touch-screen Deadbolt BE469NX CAM 619	$199	The BE469NX holds up to 30 user codes, and conveniently integrates with the Nexia Home Intelligence system. Nexia offers wireless camer-as, dimmer modules, and automated thermostats. This lock contains an anti-pick shield as well as movement sensing alarm technology.	
Kwik-set 909 Smart-code Deadbolt	$130	The 909 Smartcode Deadbolt is op-erated on 4 AA batteries, which last approximately six months (depending on usage and external tempera-tures). It is backlit for ease of use.	
iTouchless Bio-Matic BM002U	$300	The BM002U lock integrates finger-print-scanning capabilities along with a numbered touchpad. It has the capacity for 150 fingerprints and 78 unique user passcodes.	
Schlage BE365 V Cam 619	$130	This BE365 lock received the top spot in the Consumer Reports electronic door locks category. It has the capacity for 19 unique user codes, and requires no preprogramming. The mechanism does not lock automatically.	
Laykor YL-99	$59	The YL-99 is an inexpensive alterna-tive to the pricier models. It holds up to 10 user codes at once, and has LED indicators for code entry.	

Lock and key

If you do decide to retain a standard lock and key access system, here are a few tips to keep your listing running smoothly.

Firstly, make sure that you create several sets of spare keys. I'm not talking about two sets or three sets; go ahead and have *five sets* made. Does that sound excessive? Here is the method behind my madness. The first set of keys will be with you (or your space manager) at all times. That will ensure unfettered access in the case of an emergency or in the event that your presence is urgently required. You then need two sets of keys for the guests (if you want to provide true hotel-like service and convenience). That allows multiple guests to have flexibility when they go to separate locations during the day and night.

Next, you should have a fourth set as a back up. This needs to be stored somewhere in case you lose your key or you need to replace a guest key mid-stay. I recommend having a trusty neighbor keep it, so long as they are home often. And now we get to key number five, the backup key that should be stored somewhere by you (or your manager). Having a fifth key is the height of preparedness and the absolute pinnacle of forward thinking. Here's why: in the off chance that your guests happen to encounter an all-encompassing party blitz of alcohol and dance music that causes them to lose both sets of keys, you are good to go.

For starters, you can rush to their aid and provide them with key number five while retaining key number one and key number four. Next, you can scuttle down to the key store with key number one and have two extra copies made (while, once again, holding key number one). Even if you have new guests arrive before the two copies are finished, you still have a set of keys to offer them while holding onto a pair of keys yourself without disturbing key number four. Crisis averted. Bad review avoided. The day is saved. Bravo.

KEY 1	**KEY 2**	**KEY 3**	**KEY 4**	**KEY 5**
Host/	Guest	Guest	Trusty	Host/
Manager			Neighbor	Manager

Another quick tip is to make sure your lock works smoothly. If you have a lock that is tricky to open, replace it. Even if it's easy for you to open, you need to be mindful of guests who are unfamiliar with whatever magic "jiggle" or "twist" that is required to get the door to open.

Managing your space

"If you build it, [they] will come." That classic line is from *Field of Dreams*, a 1989 blockbuster about baseball and angels. This quote is a timeless piece of advice that is applicable even to the short-stay rental business. Except, of course, that it overlooks a critical piece of the Airbnb puzzle: management. Once you've set everything up in your place and it's ready for the most picky and uptight guests imaginable, you need to make sure it stays that way. Your space must be absolutely immaculate each and every time a set of new guests check-in. If you want those intricate details in place for each visitor, you need to take the time to set up a well oiled management machine.

Monitoring your listing

It is your responsibility to stay on top of your reservations. If a potential guest emails you, the onus is on you to respond in a timely fashion. Your listing's ranking is actually affected by your promptness. Accordingly, you need to keep a vigilant eye on your inbox. I recommend setting up a special filter on your email so that you can respond ASAP to any inquiry.

When I worked as a trader, I used to have a strict rule regarding work related emails: if an inquiry came in while I was awake, I would aim to respond within one hour. Responsiveness, in my opinion, is a key component of stellar customer service. Do your best of course, but my advice is to strive for a superb level of communication.

Now, if you're a traveler like me, keeping on top of your bookings can be a bit more challenging. But lo and behold, Airbnb has created an amazing way to monitor your listing on the go: the Airbnb mobile app. It doesn't matter if you're an Apple or Google loyalist; the app comes in both flavors.

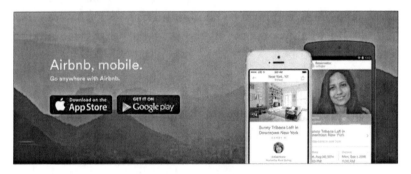

Routine cleaning

Remember: cleanliness of your property is essential, critical, necessary, vital, and an absolute must. Get my drift? Good. A survey released by J.D. Power and Associates in 2012 explored customer satisfaction (or lack thereof) in the hospitality industry. Amongst the chief complaints: lack of cleanliness. Your guests will demand a very high level of sanitation, so I recommend hiring a cleaner to prepare your space before each new guest arrives. Even if you think you are a very tidy individual, I strongly suggest employing a professional.

Instruct your cleaner to do an extremely thorough job. He should leave no stone unturned, and walk away only after the apartment is spotless and sparkling. Another quick tip: if you are giving your guests early access before the cleaning process has been completed, there is a chance that they will judge your place based on their first impressions. Translation: an act of kindness on your part might backfire. Make sure to explain to your guests that the apartment is not completely ready, and to please understand that the apartment has yet to be thoroughly cleaned.

My cleaning lady works as a maid in a five-star hotel. As you might expect, her cleaning standards are extremely high. She is an absolute perfectionist and a master of her craft. I can always trust her impeccable service and attention to detail. My recommendation to you is to put forth a few extra bucks in order to find a great cleaner. The high quality will pay dividends down the line as you accumulate five-star ratings and solid reviews.

Airbnb's pilot cleaning service

In particular regions of San Francisco, Los Angeles, and New York, Airbnb has launched its own cleaning service for select hosts. The cost for the service is $55 for a three-hour cleaning, which is taken directly from the money received for the reservation. If the reservation is canceled, the cleaning will automatically be canceled and no charges will be incurred.

Airbnb's promotional email states that the service is "affordable, easy to schedule, and can be tailored to include amenities such as linen service and gift baskets." The cleaning service targets the sections of apartments that are most critical to a happy stay. Areas that are covered include:

- **Bedrooms and common areas** – The cleaners will dust all reachable areas; wipe down surfaces and countertops; wash mirrors and glass fixtures; vacuum and mop all floors; and take out trash and recycling.

- **Bathrooms** – The cleaners will wash and wipe down toilets and basins; wash and sanitize showers and sinks; wash mirrors and glass fixtures; vacuum and mop all floors; and take out trash and recycling.

- **Kitchen** – The cleaners will wash the kitchen sink and dirty dishes; wipe down the inside and outside of the microwave; mop floors; wipe down the stove; and take out trash and recycling.

Since this new service is not available in Amsterdam, I have not been able to try it. Regardless, for folks who have access to this cleaning service, I recommend using it. Not only is it very reasonably priced, but I suspect that the quality of service is quite high (since it is backed by Airbnb).

Check-ins

Checking your guests into the unit is a critical part of the process. It's fairly simple and straightforward, but you must not bumble this part. A mishandled check-in will certainly lead to a negative review and a sour taste in your guests' mouth.

I remember staying at an apartment in Miami that was fairly nice for the price listed. I had joined a few of my friends to attend a wedding on South Beach, and I was really looking forward to spending a week in the beautiful Miami weather. But the trip was tainted from the get go. My host was irresponsible and unresponsive, and I had to wait nearly three hours before I could get inside the apartment. This caused me to be late for the wedding festivities and created a rift between the host and me. What made it worse was that the host failed to offer me a sincere apology. Needless to say, I was very disappointed and upset.

Doing it yourself

Ideally you should handle all the check-ins yourself. Although I'm on the road the majority of the year, I make sure to personally attend to my guests when I'm in town. The extra care is appreciated, and it gives me an added opportunity to learn about my guests and to optimize their experience.

If you are available during check-in, you can show your guests around the apartment and offer tips for places to visit. It is a great way to personalize the experience and ensure a solid review. And, even though this might go without saying, *always show up on time*. If you have told your guests that they can check in at noon, aim to arrive at the apartment no later than 11:45.

Once my guests have had a chance to get settled, I usually treat them for a coffee at a nearby cafe. I spend an hour or so getting to know them, answering their questions, and asking them about their plans. I don't just do this for a good review; I am genuinely interested in my guests. If you are a people person like me, I recommend adding this extra touch. It's really fun and will make your guests feel at home.

But remember, your behavior should mirror the wants and needs of each particular set of guests. If you notice that your guests are tired or perhaps a bit shy, it might be best to simply check them in and leave them be.

Outsourcing it

If you are unable to do the check-ins yourself, you will need to find a highly responsible and personable individual to do it for you. This is an important role, so choose your employee carefully.

A good candidate should be:

- Socially calibrated
- Always on standby in case of problems

- Responsible, reliable, and punctual
- In close proximity to the apartment

Obvious choices are: (1) a retired neighbor, (2) a nearby family member, or (3) a close friend. While you may have friends or family members that offer to take on this role for free, I advise against this. As the age old adage goes, "you get what you pay for." If you want someone who is reliable, friendly, and above all else, extremely professional, you should negotiate a reasonable payment.

Using a subpar employee or a friend can cost you substantially down the line. Let's say that your check-in manager forgets to show up at the apartment and isn't reachable by phone. Within an hour or two, your guests will inevitably check into a competing hotel. Once that happens, you will almost certainly lose the total rental amount. But that's just the tip of the iceberg. Your guests will leave a scathing review for everyone to see. One bad review like this could sink your listing, especially if you are just starting out. The bottom line is that your check-in manager must be at the apartment on time, every time. A no-show is simply unacceptable.

Using your cleaner to manage check-ins

If you are lucky enough to locate a personable and friendly cleaner that doesn't mind handling the check-in process, take advantage of it. I, for example, have such an arrangement with my cleaning lady. She is an awesome person, very sweet, and extremely knowledgeable about the area. It is an ideal setup as she always arranges the cleanings so that they are completed right before check-in occurs. In addition, I can always count on her in case my guests encounter a problem.

Because of her integral role and excellent service, I pay my cleaning lady well. She earns significantly more with me than she would at a normal cleaning job. Why do I do this? As I said before, "you get what you pay for." Sure, she deserves the money, but the logic behind the additional cash is so that she knows her work is appreciated. Moreover, it incentivizes her to deliver awesome service time after time.

How much do I pay her? I give her $85 per check-in. That might seem like a lot, but let me explain why it's all worth it. First off, my apartment rents for approximately $200 per night. The average guest stays approximately four nights. That's $800 per visit. $85 is about 10.6%, a reasonable cut in my opinion. And this fee doesn't just cover cleaning and a friendly face; it ensures absolute reliability in the case of any mishaps. You've lost a key? No worries, call my cleaning lady and she will be there in 15 minutes. Can't find a cool disco or café? Give her a buzz and she will point you in the right direction. My $85 ensures top-notch service with a smile. Not bad, eh?

DO THIS NOW

Write down the names of people you know who would be suitable candidates to handle your check-ins. Next, call nearby hotels and ask for recommendations from their cleaning staff. Don't tell the hotels that you are using someone for an Airbnb listing; simply state that you are looking for a part-time cleaner and would like to interview their top staff members. Compare the people you know against the interviewees and make a choice.

In addition to managing problems or answering questions, she also restocks supplies (such as toilet paper, cleaning supplies, etc.) and maintains the appliances and electronics. Since I am constantly on the go, this is an essential arrangement. It has worked out tremendously well for me, and I highly recommend it to other hosts.

Checkouts

Checking out is easy for my guests. I don't require a meet-up; instead, I simply tell them to: (1) lock the unit and (2) place the keys in the mailbox. My cleaning lady then grabs the keys when she comes over to clean. It's simple, fast, and easy. Although this strategy works reasonably well for me, I recommend that you perform a checkout if possible. Foregoing a final meet-up has several disadvantages.

First of all, guests might forget to return the keys. This has happened to me a few times. In each case, the guests had to return the keys by mail. While I was able to get the keys eventually, it took several days before they arrived. This meant that I had to entertain new guests with fewer sets.

The second disadvantage is that you are unable to locate damages before your guests leave. This can make it more difficult to open a report and ask for remuneration in the event of a mishap.

Finally, you miss the opportunity to personally interact with your guests one final time. Chatting with them as they leave is a terrific time to get honest feedback. Moreover, if there were any problems, you can tell them face to face how sorry you are and that you will immediately rectify the issues. Simply conveying that you are concerned and eager to fix the problems can bump up a rating and review.

Check-in and checkout times

I recommend following the industry standard: check-in at 3 pm and checkout by noon. It's straightforward and predictable, and it is in line with standard expectations. In addition, the three-hour buffer provides more than enough time to get the apartment spic and span.

In my experience, the majority of guests will ask for an early check-in, a late checkout, or both. My general philosophy is to accommodate my guests so long as my schedule is not adversely affected. For example, if I have a new guest checking in the same day a current guest wants a late checkout, I usually cannot oblige the request. This is because my cleaning lady needs a solid two hours to prepare the unit. I cannot risk having the apartment look subpar when my new guests arrive. When I'm unable to provide a late checkout, I refer my guests to a nearby location where they can hang out and use free WiFi. I also allow arriving guests to drop off their luggage at my apartment by noon even if the unit is still being cleaned.

Kris' Story

I used to work as a medical professional aboard massive cargo ships. My job required that I spend the majority of my time on the road, which left my four bedroom house in British Columbia, Canada, vacant for most of the year.

As you might expect, I decided to put my house up for a fixed-term rental early on in my career. I offered three of the four rooms in my house as separate rental units, each one costing $600 per month. Although I potentially could have earned a steady $1,800 per month from this setup, having full occupancy was extremely difficult to achieve. Finding people who are willing to move in with two strangers was a challenge. As a result, most months I grossed about $1,200.

During the summer of 2013, I learned of the peer-to-peer accommodations market. After a bit of research, I finally decided to launch an account on Airbnb. I was absolutely blown away by my results. During my second month of membership, I earned $1800 in just 6 nights! My returns since then have been absolutely phenomenal.

Before I learned of Airbnb, I felt that my only option was to live with roommates. Additionally, because my work required me to travel frequently, if I wasn't renting to roommates, I would often find myself paying the entire mortgage on an empty house.

Since transitioning to a short-stay rental model, my life has changed drastically. Because of the extra income I've earned, I am now self-employed and pursuing a career that I'm truly passionate about. I rent my house out when I'm working away from home, mostly to vacationers, families, and businessmen. If a group is interested in renting the house when I am scheduled to be home, I simply extend my travel plans and enjoy myself abroad knowing that my mortgage is being paid for.

But, not only am I paying my mortgage, I'm cash-flowing every month and earning a bunch of extra money with a greater than 70% occupancy rate. This gives me the freedom to travel and spend my time how I want, where I want, and with the people I love. That, to me, is the definition of freedom.

As far as I'm concerned, short-stay rentals are the way to go. They give you much more flexibility with your property. If you take the time to set up a solid listing, I'm confident that you can make significantly more money than you would with a long-term lease. Plus you are insured through the Airbnb guarantee, which protects your house in the event of any damages. Add in the fact that you can still use your house whenever you want to, and the short-term path just makes the most sense.

In December of last year, I rented my house to a family during the holidays. I charged a significant premium for the dates they stayed because of the heightened demand. While the house was rented, I traveled to Western Canada to see my parents. Of course, staying at my parents' house was virtually free (aside from helping out with groceries and buying them dinner), so I was able to save most of the money I made on the rental. After a relaxing visit with Mom and Dad, I traveled to Mexico and spent two weeks on the beach with some friends. We did nothing but swim in the ocean, work out at the gym, lie on the beach, surf, and check out the local pubs. The money I made from renting my house over the holidays paid for my mortgage and more than covered the expense of my vacation. And that's just one amazing story. The bottom line is that I'm now able to work about half of the year and vacation the other half. Life is amazing.

CHAPTER 2

Creating a Killer Listing

"Many a small thing has been made large by the right kind of advertising."

- Mark Twain, Author

et's say your rental space is in a major world city that has a long list of eager tourists. Cool. Let's also say that your space resides in the heart of that city in the most vibrant and upscale section. Great. Let's also assume that your apartment is gorgeous, each room is cleaned to perfection, and the amenities are top notch. Fantastic. But guess what? It's all for naught if your listing fails to captivate potential guests. You can cross every "t" and dot every "i" ad infinitum, but if you neglect your Airbnb listing, your short-stay rental career will most certainly end in failure.

Creating a solid listing is essential for yielding inquiries and bookings. Your listing is a one shot opportunity to tell your story, describe your space, and answer any anticipated questions. It is a golden tablet upon which you can establish your brand and convey your quality. The Nielson Norman Group reports that average web users stay on a particular website for a duration of 10-20 seconds. That's not even enough time to read one page of a standard novel! Translation: you'll be lucky if the average Airbnb user spends more than 5-10 seconds on your listing. Accordingly, you need to pack as much of a punch as possible.

Renting your space as an "entire home/apartment," "private room," or "shared room"

When creating your custom listing, the first thing you must decide is how you want to sell your space. You can either: (1) offer it at as a complete unit or (2) rent it out piecemeal to multiple parties at once. The options for listing your space are as follows:

- **Entire home/apartment** – This option involves renting out your entire home to a single group of guests. It is most akin to a hotel stay.

- **Private room** – With this option, you can offer each individual room as a distinct rental property. For example, if you own a three-bedroom apartment, you may rent each bedroom to separate guests for the same period of time. Multiple groups of guests will then have to share the common areas.

- **Shared room** – This allows guests to share a single room with other travelers, much like the sleeping arrangements found in hostels. This is especially popular amongst folks who are roaming the globe on a budget.

Choosing the right option will depend on your personal circumstances. For example, if you live in the space you are renting, or only own a studio or a one bedroom, you will likely have to market your space as either a "private room" or a "shared room."

Personally, I have only rented my apartment as an "entire home/apartment." If you have the capacity to select this option, I recommend doing so. You won't have to deal with potential quarrels between different groups of guests, and your liabilities will be easier to manage.

Pictures

One of the most hackneyed phrases in the English language is "a picture is worth 1,000 words." Most children in elementary school are familiar with the saying and understand its meaning. In short, human beings are highly visual animals. We rely primarily on our acute vision to understand the world. The sense of sight is our key tool to hunt animals, decode history, create technology, and understand our fellow human beings. If anything, a picture is worth far more than 1,000 words.

In line with this foundational principle, the first part of your listing that any visitor will scrutinize is your assortment of photos. When the search results populate, users will see your title and the accompanying primary photo. This is the most critical factor of your click through rate (CTR). As such, make sure your place looks its absolute best when conducting the photo shoot.

When it comes to the actual photo shoot, I strongly recommend that you take advantage of Airbnb's professional photo service. If it is available in your area, use it. According to Airbnb, hosts that use this service make on average two and a half times as much income as hosts who use their own photos. Oh, I almost forgot to mention… the professional photo service is absolutely free! Moreover, the photographers are highly professional and manage the entire photo shoot themselves.

A week or two after the shoot, you will have a lovely collection of pictures uploaded directly to your listing. You are then free to add captions and descriptions.

Before your space is photographed, make sure to:

- Clean the house thoroughly
- Put away any stray items
- Keep wires out of sight
- Use your best linens

If the photo service is unavailable and you must take the pictures yourself, here are a few tips from professional photographers:

- Optimize the lighting
- Try to use only natural light
- Take the pictures during the early morning or late afternoon so that the sunlight is less direct
- Keep the lighting consistent from room to room
- Adjust the focus of the camera to make sure that the details of the room are sharp
- Use a tripod so that you can take advantage of a longer exposure time without sacrificing the clarity of the image
- Take low shots, approximately 40 inches off the ground, to replicate the feel of magazine style shots
- Shoot straight on without any tilt; modifying the angles can distort lines
- Avoid wide-angle lenses
- Turn off your flash

Once you have assembled your collection of photos, make sure to *assign the best and most descriptive photo as your primary photo.* Good primary photos are usually shots of the living room or other large areas that reflect the best features of your space. Here's the primary photo that I use for my listing.

Once you have added enough photos to cover all of the pertinent rooms and amenities in your space, add some good pictures of the most interesting features of your neighborhood. Try including a photo of a busy café, a nearby park, and a bustling pub.

For every picture, make sure to include a colorful and descriptive caption. Mention the best features of each room so as to guide the eyes of your potential guests.

5/17: The kitchen is fully equipped with a dish washer, oven, fridge, espresso machine, and everything you need to cook a great meal!

7/17: The master bedroom is equipped with a TV, an air conditioning unit, a DVD player, and a large closet

Profile

Renting a house is a personal and intimate arrangement for both parties. Homes are the physical embodiment of personal space and territory, and inviting a stranger into that world is an enormous leap of faith requiring a healthy amount of implicit trust. Likewise, stepping into another's home can intrinsically trigger a feeling of awkwardness and discomfort. Humans are creatures of habit, and familiarity is a central component of our comfort.

In order to assuage this natural instinct, it is imperative that you allow your potential guests to get to know you on a personal level. The profile is your opportunity to show your true colors and let passersby develop a virtual bond with you. It will ease their minds and make them more likely to reach out to you regarding your space.

Make sure to fill out every detail of your profile. Describe your occupation, hobbies, and general music/movie preferences. You never know which precise piece of your profile will catch a user's eye, so it is important to be as detailed and thorough as possible.

Finally, Airbnb allows you to record and display a short 30-second video of yourself. Even though most visitors won't bother watching the video, I recommend that you take the time to film one. Why? Because it can be the clinching factor for those visitors want to see your personality live and in color.

Personal photo

Make sure to upload a good picture of yourself. What is a good picture? Here are the key characteristics:

- The picture is clear and of high quality
- You are smiling
- Your face and eyes are unobstructed
- Your hair is combed/brushed
- Your outfit is business casual

For those of you out there who consider this information common sense: Bravo. But I cannot tell you how many profile pictures I've come across that fail to meet these basic criteria. I've seen photos with covered faces, bizarre and inappropriate outfits, and utterly creepy looking expressions. Please, for your own sake, don't look like a weirdo.

Creating your Airbnb Symbol

In an effort to offer a more personalized experience, Airbnb provides hosts the opportunity to generate a self-made symbol to represent their particular brand. This is a fun way to get creative and express yourself. Additionally, it gives potential guests another means by which to understand you and your home. The website has an easy to use symbol editor that allows hosts to modify color schemes, change designs, and add an assortment of images.

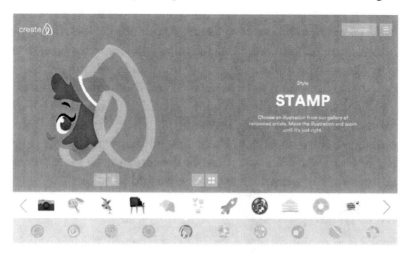

Title and description

Before you choose a title and description, take a moment to consider your prime audience. Essentially, you need to think about the types of people that would be attracted to your apartment and location. Do you live in a quiet neighborhood with nearby parks? Your space could be a draw for families or older folks. Is your apartment a posh pad within close proximity to the city's most choice nightlife options? It might be considered a gem by weekend warriors and hard partying young professionals. Does your home have an awe-inspiring view and a cozy feel? It could provide a perfect getaway for hot and heavy couples.

The core idea is to unleash a targeted marketing campaign. If you try and appeal to everyone, you'll likely reel in no one. My apartment, for example, has two bedrooms on opposite sides separated by a communal area and a staircase. This barrier creates a lot of privacy for my guests, which makes my apartment ideal for multiple couples traveling together. As such, I exploit this unique aspect in my title: "Perfect couples home! 2-bdr getaway."

Additionally, you can use your title as a filter for the types of guests you want to attract. If you prefer hosting elderly couples, deploy a title that would seem inviting to that particular group like "Quiet Getaway For Couples."

Your title

Every marketable product has a title. The revolutionary phone released by Apple was dubbed the "iPhone." The groundbreaking television series about a cancer ridden high school chemistry teacher was called "Breaking Bad." The iconic sandwich that has been served to billions of people across the globe was named the "Big Mac." Successful products have good titles, and although substance is important, a clever or catchy name can mean the difference between a customer trying something new or passing up an amazing product.

Your title needs to be snappy, inviting, and specially tailored for a particular crowd. It needs to prompt users to click and explore your listing. I recommend using descriptive terms and phraseology such as "perfect location," "luxurious," or "incredible amenities." Think about the best and most unique aspects of your house and try to incorporate them into your title.

A good title should accomplish two goals: it should: (1) grab the users attention and (2) provide some key information regarding the space. Now, I've seen many titles that include either the city name or the particular neighborhood. These are both improper uses of the title. Why? Because both the city and neighborhood are prominently displayed in the search results.

Here is a table of great titles from different cities. All of these listings are amongst the highest performers within their locales.

Title	City
Luxury Priv Beachside Studio, Pool	Los Angeles
Beautiful Studio in Luxury Building	New York
Artsy Artist's Studio by the Lake	Chicago
Amenity Rich Condo Downtown/Parking	Vancouver
Stunning Art Lovers Rock'nRoll Apt!	Toronto
Luxury Quiet Close To Eiffel Tower	Paris
Chic and Cosy flat near Big Ben.	London
3BR FOR 8 IN DOWTOWN WIFI AC	Madrid
City Center Bohemian Apartment	Rome
Danube Deluxe Design Apartment	Budapest
SPACIOUS MODERN APT & AMAZING VIEW	Hvar
Central, spacious & quiet room (L)	Stockholm
2br Luxury Apt 1 Block from Beach	Rio Di Janeiro
The Best Place To Live BuenosAires!	Buenos Aires
Elegant Penthouse - Dazzling View	Medellin
High-Floor Apt with Beautiful Views	Santiago
Superb 2br pool villa-Amazing view!	Bali
Walk to Roppongi with mobile wifi	Tokyo
Hip French Concession 1BR + Bike&VPN	Shanghai
HONEYMOONERvilla w/complete privacy	Phuket

A great way to drive up business and customer demand is to modify your title based on the season. Since bookings usually happen within one to two months of a guest's travel date, you can modify your title temporally in accordance with whatever major event is about to take place. Just take a moment to consider what events or seasons tend to draw the largest crowds from out of town. Here are two illustrative examples.

- **Kings Day,** Amsterdam – The celebration of the King's birthday is literally called "King's Day." Not very creative, I know, but nonetheless, it attracts loads of tourists from Europe and the Americas. If my place is still available a few weeks before the event, I change the title of my listing to one of the following options:
  - "Perfect location for King's Day"
  - "King's Day Central Celebration"
  - "2BR Luxury King's Day Space"

- **Carnival,** Rio de Janeiro – Carnival in Brazil is known as one of the wildest parties on the planet. Visitors head to Rio in droves so that they can partake in the non-stop festivities. A few examples of good titles are as follows:
  - "2BR Luxury Carnival Center Parties"
  - "Watch Carnival Parade from Balcony"
  - "Best Spot Carnival"

Your description

If you have successfully drawn in a potential customer with your awesome pictures and title, the description is where you seal the deal. This is your opportunity to paint a picture of your home, its amenities, and the surrounding area with a lovely palette of words. I encourage you to sink your teeth into this section and let your writing answer any hanging questions or concerns a potential guest might have.

Items to include in the description are:

- The size of the house (square feet)
- Number of bedrooms
- Number of bathrooms
- Any outdoor area (e.g. balconies, patios, porches, etc.)
- Description of rooms
- The floor you are on (e.g. ground level, top floor, etc.)
- Presence of an elevator
- Proximity to public transport
- Proximity to supermarkets
- Parking availability

Again, this is your chance to be detailed and elaborative. Give your reader every last bit of pertinent information you can muster. What size are the beds? What appliances does your kitchen have? Is there a bathtub in the bathrooms, or just a shower? While the "title" is like your diploma, a piece of paper with the name of your major, the description is your PhD thesis, an in-depth rundown of everything you have to offer.

Finally, when you are describing your apartment and its amenities, employ wording that evokes positive emotions. Instead of simply describing furniture and items in a matter-of-fact way, attempt to use colorful words and phrases.

Poor Wording	Good Wording
"The house has a balcony."	"After a great day of sightseeing, the balcony is a perfect and lush spot to reflect on the day while enjoying a cool drink in the afternoon sun."
"My apartment has a bedroom, a bathroom, and a full kitchen with utensils and cooking materials."	"Notice the meticulous decoration in this immaculately clean apartment. The space is comprised of a cozy double-bedroom, a large and well lit bathroom, an impressively chic living room, and a fully stocked kitchen that is perfect for any amateur chef looking to prepare a delicious meal!"
"This apartment is my former home, and I took the time to make it my own. I bought new appliances and updated the fittings myself."	"This apartment used to be my personal home. As a result, the space is not simply a bland unit without character or imagination; instead, it has a carefully designed interior with quality fittings and appliances. There is an aura of tranquility that will make your stay in London a special one."
"The house has a lovely deck area with seats and a barbecue grill. There is even an AstroTurf covering."	"As you exit the apartment through the French doors at the rear of the kitchen, you'll find a quiet oasis in a busy city: a fully finished deck area with numerous seating options and an AstroTurf meadow. It is the ideal spot for a barbecue party on a warm summer night."

Although you want your listing to be as attractive and appealing as possible, make sure to give an accurate and realistic presentation. *Don't promise things you can't deliver.* To ensure that you are providing a well-tailored and reasonably representative listing, Airbnb has a special rating category called "Accuracy." If you push the limits and mislead your customers, your overall rating will pay the price.

35 Reviews ★ ★ ★ ★ ★

Summary				
	Accuracy	★ ★ ★ ★ ★	Location	★ ★ ★ ★ ★
	Communication	★ ★ ★ ★ ★	Check In	★ ★ ★ ★ ★
	Cleanliness	★ ★ ★ ★ ★	Value	★ ★ ★ ★ ★

It's better to under-promise and over-deliver than the other way around. This might cost you a few bookings in the short-term, but the excellent "Accuracy" reviews will bolster your reputation down the line and solidify your opportunity to turn your listing into a sustainable investment vehicle.

For example, if you have a reasonably fast Internet connection, don't refer to it as high speed. If you do, people who actually *need* high speed Internet for business reasons will specifically choose your place on this basis. Guess what happens when your customers realize that your connection is not what they expected? Your review will be devastating. And not just for the "Accuracy" rating… the negative emotions will likely spill into the other ratings as well. But that's a best-case scenario. Truly perturbed guests who are relying completely on a speedy connection could very well leave, in which case you might have to refund their money in full.

Lastly, remember that we are living in an age of short-form content. People want their information quickly and in small, digestible chunks. Accordingly, make sure to front-load your description with the most pertinent information. Take the time to go into detail, but bear in mind that an impatient reader might only skim the first third of your description. To make everyone happy, organize your writing so that the most important bits are at the top.

House rules

If you want to be a happy host, you will need your guests to respect your home. In order to ensure that your place is treated well and in accordance with your particular specifications, it is wise to establish a set of "House Rules." This is not meant to be a collection of obvious and uninviting regulations; instead, it is supposed to encapsulate neighborhood or building rules that new guests might be unaware of. For example, if the next-door neighbor has asked that no music be played after 11 pm, you should likely include that. Or if the building prohibits smoking on your balcony, you should mention that as well. Let your guests know precisely what rules need to be followed. This will improve the overall experience for both parties.

Minimum and maximum amount of nights

Airbnb gives you the option to set a minimum and maximum amount of nights for potential guests. You'll find that a lot of highly visited apartments set a two or three night minimum. This is to maximize profits and reduce hassles.

If, however, you are a new user with few reviews, I recommend setting the minimum to one night. Why? Well, to be frank, beggars can't be choosers. Your doors should be wide open at the onset of your Airbnb career so that you can effectively build your brand. The initial goal is to simply secure as many good reviews and high ratings as possible so that you can climb up the rankings ladder.

When it comes to setting a maximum amount of nights, I recommend keeping it to one week, especially for newbies. The goal is to keep the rentals flowing while still providing ample time for a full vacation. Even for seasoned users, increasing the maximum doesn't make much sense. Why? Ideally, your price should be fixed at a point where guests find it too expensive to book your apartment for two weeks or a month. If your apartment is in high demand by folks seeking lengthy stays, your price is set too low.

Cancellation policy

Airbnb provides five cancellation policy options:

1. **Flexible** – Guests are entitled to a full refund **one day** prior to arrival.

2. **Moderate** – Guests are entitled to a full refund **five days** prior to arrival.

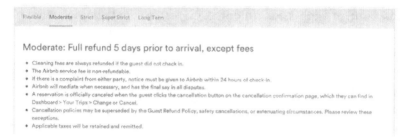

3. **Strict** – Guests are entitled to a **50% refund** up until **one week** prior to arrival.

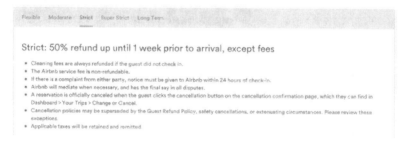

4. **Super Strict** – Guests are entitled to a **50% refund** up until **30 days** prior to arrival.

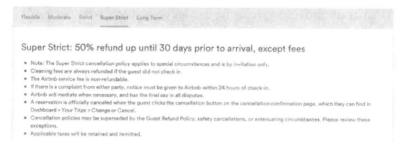

5. **Long Term** – First month down payment is required; **30 days** notice is necessary for lease termination.

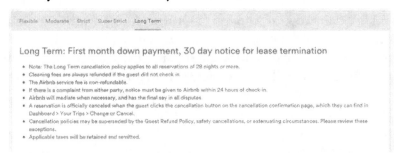

If you are new to Airbnb, I recommend choosing the **Flexible** policy. From a consumer standpoint, the Flexible option is by far the easiest and simplest way to make a reservation. It will encourage users to choose your apartment despite a lack of reviews. Also, when you are new and your bookings are fairly sparse, a last minute cancellation won't affect you significantly. This is only a major concern for heavily sought apartments that face a much higher opportunity cost for canceled visits

Once you've reached approximately 80%+ occupancy, you can consider switching to Moderate. At this point, you presumably have a stable reputation. Translation: you can afford to dissuade the flakier customers simply because the level of demand is high enough. Moreover, at this level of occupancy, cancellations will significantly impact your earning power. If you're unsure of whether or not to switch to Moderate, take a look at your cancellations over the last three months. If you are getting a high percentage of cancellations, somewhere in the neighborhood of 20%, I would recommend switching to Moderate.

With respect to Strict, Super Strict, and Long Term, I advise against all of these policies (unless warranted by a state regulation or building policy). They are highly restrictive and quite unpleasant from a consumer standpoint. When is the last time you ever heard of a hotel enforce such strict regulations? It is completely out of whack with hospitality industry standards. Additionally, if you are indeed looking to lease your space on a long-term basis, you will likely be best served on an apartment rental website.

Creating a custom made guidebook

Guidebooks are your opportunity to add a personal touch and a creative flair. You can convey: (1) instructions on where to find appliances and knickknacks in your house, (2) neighborhood preferences, (3) favorite local afternoon activities, and (4) special nightlife hot spots. This is your chance to shine above and beyond any well-known hotel chain. Sure, the internationally recognized five-star hotels have polished and professional concierges, but these folks are often caught in the tricky position of wanting to offer sincere advice and having to point you in the direction of partnered restaurants and bars. These corporate strictures don't apply to you. You are your own entity, and guests can be assured that whatever advice you offer will be pure and untainted.

Once the reservation has been booked, shoot over a PDF copy of your guidebook. In addition, print out two copies and place them in the living room area. The more professional it looks, the better. Feel free to add color and a special binder, but bear in mind that these guidebooks usually have a short lifespan as they are subject to a reasonable amount of wear and tear.

The guidebook should contain at least three sections:

- The house/apartment
- The neighborhood
- Practical information

The value of local advice is unparalleled. Travelers relish any opportunity to glean guidance from a born and raised native. So again, please take advantage of this wonderfully powerful tool. Not only will it be highly useful, but it will likely be appreciated by your guests in the form of positive reviews.

The house/apartment

This section is used to explain the basic layout of the apartment. In addition, this is a great opportunity to walk your guests through the operation of your appliances. Again, don't assume that your gadgets are as intuitive as you might imagine. Using a blender for the first time can be confusing without access to an instruction manual. Items to include within this portion of the guidebook are:

- **Electricity** – Describe the location of the outlets and the circuit breaker

- **Television** – Explain how to use the remote, how to access cable, and how to operate the DVD player; provide a list of channels

- **Heating** – Show: (1) where the thermostat is located and (2) how to operate it

- **Keys** – Give a quick rundown of how to use the various keys

- **Shower** – Tell your guests how to operate the shower/bath

- **Kitchen & Cooking** – Explain how to use all major appliances (such as the stove, microwave, toaster, dishwasher, etc.) and show the location of utensils and cooking materials

- **Garbage** – Describe where the garbage is, where extra garbage bags can be found, and where refuse is to be placed

- **Laundry** – Show your guests: (1) where the laundry machines or closest laundromats are located, (2) how to operate them, (3) and where detergent and dryer sheets can be found

- **Smoking** – Specify the smoking conditions in your space (e.g. no smoking, smoking on the balcony only, etc.)

- **Noise** – Provide your guests with the general noise guidelines (e.g. no loud music after 10 pm, keep conversation low after 11 pm, etc.)

- **Parties** – Specify whether or not parties or outside guests are permitted in your space

- **Parking** – Explain where parking spots can be located for visitors with cars

- **Checklist for checkout** – Give your guests a list of items to check before turning over the keys and walking out the door (e.g. confirm that the gas is shut off, the lights are off, the door is locked, etc.)

The neighborhood

Here is your chance to provide that wonderful local insight. You've frequented the bars, sampled the restaurants, and loitered in the cafes for years and years. Accordingly, you are an expert of your city. Soak that in for a moment. Yes, you are indeed an expert. This is your opportunity to share your valuable insight with knowledge thirsty newcomers.

If you want to provide really stellar service, I recommend making a list of cool attractions or restaurants with: (1) an accompanying photo, (2) an address and map screenshot, (3) a link to the menu (if the location serves food), and (4) the best day/ time to visit. Items to include are as follows:

- Restaurants
- Pubs and discos
- Taxi numbers
- Public transport locations
- Popular malls and shops
- Nearby grocery stores
- Pharmacies
- Tourist attractions

Practical information

For all intents and purposes, this is your "miscellaneous" section. It is a catchall for pieces of random information that might come in handy. You can include things like: (1) what to do in case of an emergency, (2) information about medical services, (3) who to contact in case of apartment related problems, and (4) how to have late night food delivered.

Creating an official "Airbnb Guidebook"

Airbnb provides hosts with the option to create a guidebook within the Airbnb platform. You can find this option on the "Manage Listing" page (see image below).

This page offers a convenient way to make recommendations to your guests. You can add cafes, restaurants, tourist attractions, and anything that might tickle the fancy of a potential guest. If you have created an Airbnb Guidebook, it will be viewable when guests scroll down through your listing.

Michael's Story

I have worked in San Francisco for the last few years at a competitive technology company. My life has been very busy, and I often find myself working more than 80 hours a week.

One nice work perk is that I get to travel a ton, nearly two weeks out of every month. As nice as it is to visit new locations, I quickly became frustrated that I was spending $2,650 per month on rent while only sleeping in my apartment half of the time. So after speaking with a number of friends and satisfied Airbnb customers, I finally decided to give Airbnb a shot. I am pleased to say that I haven't had a single bad experience. More importantly, I am able to recoup a large share of the rent I pay each month. And, as an added bonus, I'm more inclined to go out of town on weekends for fun because I know that I can easily recoup the money I spend on flights.

I started renting my apartment for just $150 per night and have quickly gone up to $200. I have noticed that the demand is still high, so I will probably hike the rent up to $250 per night.

I've found Airbnb to be incredibly simple, straightforward, and easy to use. It prompted me for answers about my space that were later used to make up my profile. There are tons of customizable options that help me filter potential guests so that I can minimize risk and maximize profits. They even sent over complimentary photographers to take photos of my apartment! It really couldn't be easier, and I couldn't be happier.

CHAPTER 3

Pricing

*"What is a cynic?
A man who knows the
price of everything
and the value of nothing."*

- Oscar Wilde, Author

When attempting to achieve success in any business, creating an awesome product is a baseline requirement. Once a product is finalized, marketing is the next step. The goal of a solid marketing campaign is to: (1) make your product look amazing and (2) display your product to as many potential consumers as possible. But sandwiched between these two steps is a critical question that must be answered with great care: *how much should this product cost?*

This is a more complex question than you might think, one that has confused and befuddled many bright minds. Economists have espoused several basic price-setting strategies. One approach is to set the price based on cost (a.k.a. "Gross Profit Margin Target"). If the average cost of a widget is $3.00, it ostensibly makes sense to price it at $3.30. That's a 10% profit per widget sold. Sounds reasonable. But you could also look at what competitors are charging for similar products and create a price based on that information (a.k.a. "Competitor-Based Pricing"). Also a logical approach. Or you could set the price according to the maximum amount a consumer would pay for your product (a.k.a. "What The Market Will Bear"). That makes sense too. So what's the right approach? Moreover how do you go about determining cost, comparable products, and the actual dollar amount that people are willing to pay for your product?

These are truly difficult questions to answer. The best employable strategy will vary from product to product and across industry spectrums. The same is true of Airbnb listings. The optimal pricing strategy for a particular listing will depend on the relative luxuriousness, location, and overall appeal of your apartment. Finding the best pricing strategy isn't easy and will require a great deal of experimentation.

Although choosing the right price seems to be a daunting task, the following section will help you parse the available information so that you have the best chance of determining the perfect price in the least amount of time.

Finding an optimal pricing strategy

Finding an optimal pricing strategy isn't easy. In fact, it's not even mathematically possible. There are simply too many unpredictable and unknown variables to realistically identify all of the pertinent facts and criteria. But don't fret just yet... this section is full of helpful observations that will guide you as effectively and efficiently as possible so that you can cross this seemingly gaping chasm unscathed. I will set up a logical framework within which you can tinker and experiment until you unlock your optimal price point. By utilizing the age-old learning tool of "trial and error," you will eventually derive a solid pricing strategy.

First things first... what is an "optimal pricing strategy?" The definition I am using is a pricing strategy that *maximizes profit in the long run*. You don't need an economics degree to understand this concept. It literally means the strategy that makes the most cash!

Before I dive into this quest, let's start off with same basic profit theory. First off, profit is defined as follows:

Profit = Revenue (R) - Total Costs (TC)

Revenue is the money that Airbnb will pay you on behalf of your guests. *Total Costs* are the amount of money you expend on behalf of your listing. Total costs can be subdivided into two distinct parts: (1) fixed costs and (2) marginal costs.

Total Costs (TC) = Fixed Costs (FC) + Marginal Costs (MC)

Fixed Costs are expenses that are not dependent on the amount of days your place is occupied. You will incur these costs regardless of reservations or number of guests. Examples of fixed costs for a listing are: (1) mortgage payments, (2) property taxes, (3) rent, (4) building maintenance, (5) condominium fees, and (6) TV/internet subscriptions.

Marginal Costs are expenses that will be incurred based on usage. As the number of guests increase, the marginal costs will rise. Examples of these costs are: (1) electricity, (2) gas, (3) water, and (4) management costs.

Management costs include everything that must be paid to organize a stay at your house, such as: (1) cleaning, (2) managing check-ins/checkouts, and (3) acquiring basic supplies for your listing. If you hire someone to fulfill these roles, the cost is whatever you pay that person. If you tend to these tasks yourself, then you calculate this value according to your opportunity cost (i.e. how much money you could have made doing something else during the same time). If you charge your guests an extra cleaning fee, then the cleaning cost drops out of the equation.

Although your fixed costs partly define the magnitude of your profit, they shouldn't influence your pricing strategy. This is because your fixed costs are a given; they are not dependent on the amount of days you rent your place out.

This leads to the first concrete conclusion:

The optimal pricing strategy is independent of fixed costs.

To illustrate this conclusion, consider the following example:

Let's assume that you rent out your space full time and have no other use for it. In other words, you don't gain anything if it's empty.

Now let's assume that your fixed costs are as follows:

Mortgage =	$1000/month
TV/Internet =	$100/month
Insurance =	$50/month
Local Taxes =	$150/month
Routine Maintenance =	$200/month
Total Fixed Costs =	**$1500/month**
	= $50/day

Marginal costs (assuming your space is occupied) are as follows:

Gas/Water/Electricity =	$300/month
Miscellaneous Supplies =	$300/month
Management Costs =	$150/month
Variable Maintenance =	$150/month
Total Marginal Costs =	**$900/month**
	= $30/day

Now consider the following options:

Option 1: Rent out your space for $40 for a particular day

Option 2: Leave your place unoccupied

Option 1

If you rent out your place for $40 a day, you technically won't be putting money in your bank account. Why? Because you are spending $50 alone in fixed costs. Taking on guests will drop you another $30 in the hole for that day, bringing the grand total of expenditures to $80. That means for that particular day, you will lose $40.

Option 2

If you leave your house empty, you don't incur any marginal costs. But, you still must pay the fixed costs of $50 per day. That's a total expenditure of $50.

The inevitable conclusion is that although Option 1 leaves you at a loss, it is superior to Option 2.

Therefore, the second observation is:

As long as your price is higher than your marginal costs, you are better off renting your space out than leaving it empty.

This means that the lowest price you should accept is equal to your marginal costs, which in this case is $30. This is the lowest bound of the price range for any given day. Even though you are making no money at this point, you are still getting the benefit of ratings and reviews, which will lead to more bookings in the future.

Now, let's say you can successfully rent your space for $40 per day, but you've decided that $10 per day of net profit ($40 - $30) isn't worth your time. Fair enough, but what profit margin will satisfy you? $20? $30? Determine what value suits your fancy and readjust your management costs. For example, if the minimum you are willing to accept is $30 per day, your management costs will move from $5 to $35 per day. The lower bound of your price now shifts to $60.

Now that we have figured out how to identify the lower bound, let's address the far more complex problem: what is the maximum price a potential set of guests might pay? What does this price depend on?

To answer these questions, I must assume the perspective of my potential guests. How does the decision making process work from a consumer standpoint? First, I will presume that my imaginary guests have made the decision to stay in my neighborhood. As such, they will search the available neighborhood options and choose the apartment that fits them best.

When contemplating an optimal price for these guests, I will consider the prices of the best alternatives to my house. If my neighbor has a similar house and it is available for $100 per night, no reasonable guest will pay $200 for my space. However, would this imaginary set of guests pay $130? Or $120? Possibly. There could be arbitrary differences that serendipitously mesh with the guests' personal tastes or preferences. Assuming they have the money to spend, these guests might pay a slight premium to enjoy the pleasant colors of my wall, the arrangement of my living room, or the high-end coffee machine in my kitchen.

This brings me to the third observation:

Your maximum price is equal to the price of the best alternative in your neighborhood plus a certain margin to allow for personal preferences.

So what is this magical margin? Great question. The reality is that you won't be able to determine that margin right away. The only way to decipher this golden number is via experimentation. You must put on a scientist's hat and engage in a price setting experiment. It is your job to monitor the prices you set and the corresponding requests for lodging.

Let's assume that after reviewing a number of listings, I conclude that the best alternatives cost $200. Let's further assume that I have decided to add an arbitrary 25% margin on top, which gives me a maximum price of $250.

I now have a price range for my apartment: **$30 - $250**

The next question is: how do I choose a price within this range for any given point in time? Recognize that the price will vary considering where you are on the timeline. Let's consider a few points in time: T+90 (90 days from the current date), T+7 (7 days from the current date), and T+1 (one day from current date).

First, let's consider what price might make sense at T+90. Since I am 90 days away from the booking date, it makes sense to price my apartment at $250 for this time range. The goal is to give potential guests who are willing to pay the maximum price a lengthy time frame in which to make a reservation. Since I have over 12 weeks to find guests, losing a booking due to a high price is less detrimental.

What happens as I approach T+0 (the current date)? As the booking date comes closer to the present date, the probability of finding guests who are willing to pay the maximum price decreases. This increases the chance that my place will be left empty, which, as I've already established, isn't a good option.

Accordingly, it makes sense to lower my price as I get closer to T+0. The basic theory is that as my risk level of vacancy increases, I should proportionately reduce the price to mitigate that risk. This price will continue to drop from $250 all the way down to my lower bound, $30.

Now let's consider T+7 (one week from the current date). Over the last 11 weeks, I've lowered my price from $250 to $100, but I still haven't found any guests. Since there is very little time left and the risk of my apartment being unused is relatively high, I will apply a drastic price cut and reduce the nightly rate to $75.

At T+1 (one day from the current date), I have almost no time left to find any guests. At this point, I refer back to the weathered adage: "beggars can't be choosers." Translation: I will lower my price to the minimum of $30.

This brings me to the fourth observation:

You should apply your maximum price point for far off check-in dates; as check-in dates approach the current date, the price should be lowered up until the minimum price point.

How long in advance should I start lowering my price from the maximum? Once again, only experimentation will shine a light on this answer. From personal experience, I recommend using three months (T+90) as the upper bound of the test dates.

To illustrate how to implement this strategy, take a look at the table below:

Time from current date	Price
Beyond 12 weeks	$250
12 weeks	$225
11 weeks	$225
10 weeks	$225
9 weeks	$225
8 weeks	$200
7 weeks	$200
6 weeks	$175
5 weeks	$175
4 weeks	$150
3 weeks	$125
2 weeks	$100
1 week	$75
A few days	$30

Future profits

Even if you rent out your house for $30, you are still better off in the long run. Why? Because of potential future profits resulting from the aggregate reviews and ratings you will accumulate. In addition, previous guests might return at a later time and/or recommend your space to others.

When you begin your Airbnb career, it makes sense to rent your space for a price near the marginal cost. This is because reviews are especially valuable and impactful early on. For example, one review versus no reviews is a very substantial difference, whereas 21 reviews versus 20 reviews is not nearly as significant of a bump.

This leads me to observation number five:

The fewer reviews you have, the more aggressively you should lower your price as the check-in date draws closer to the current date.

Summary

Although calculating an optimal price is a highly complex endeavor, I have outlined five global rules that can efficiently guide you through the pricing matrix:

1. *The optimal pricing strategy is independent of fixed costs.*

2. *As long as your price is higher than your marginal costs, you are better off renting your space out than leaving it empty.*

3. *Your maximum price is equal to the price of the best alternative in your neighborhood plus a certain margin to allow for personal preferences.*

4. *You should apply your maximum price point for far off check-in dates; as check-in dates approach the current date, the price should be lowered until the minimum price point.*

5. *The fewer reviews you have, the more aggressively you should lower your price as the check-in date draws closer to the current date.*

Experimenting

Learning the premium margin that you can charge will take dedicated practice, observation, and analysis. For example, let's say it's January and your maximum price is $250. For April and beyond, set one week at $300, one at $275, one at $250, and one at $225. Observe your bookings and record the data. Create an Excel spreadsheet to keep track of: (1) what point in time bookings are made and (2) at what price. After enough practice, you'll identify patterns and hone your strategy.

New listings

When you are just starting out, your main priorities should be:

- Building your reputation within the Airbnb community
- Improving your listing's visibility in the search results

If you focus on these two priorities, you will maximize your long-term income. As I've already established, you should be willing to accept very low prices early on. The focus should be on trying to get as many bookings as possible to build your reputation.

Now, if you are pricing your apartment very low, considerably lower than comparable apartments, you should include a reason for the low price in your description. For example, you can state something like "30% discount, this month only, for my first ten guests!" If you don't offer an explanation, people might assume that there is something wrong with your home.

Adjusting prices to match fluctuating demand

Every city in the world has high seasons and low seasons for tourists. People love to travel to European cities in the summer, tropical regions in the winter, and culturally vibrant locales during seasonal festivals and celebrations. As demand waxes and wanes, you should take notice and adjust your prices accordingly. Personally, I maintain a three season pricing schedule for my place in Amsterdam:

- Low season (November through February)
- Medium season (March through May and September through October)
- High season (June through August)

The prices I use for low/medium/high season are approximately 60%/80%/100%.

Peak periods

You must be cognizant of stark demand deviations that occur during special holidays such as Christmas and New Years. Also, be on the lookout for large corporate conferences that take place in nearby convention centers. The Consumer Electronics Show in Las Vegas brings in approximately 150,000 visitors each year. Conferences like this attract enormous waves of well-to-do business people looking to spend some serious coin on accommodations. More importantly, the hotels will likely be overbooked and overpriced, making a pleasant Airbnb rental very enticing.

Depending on the event, you might be able to earn double the normal price or more. An excellent way to gauge demand is to search for a hotel on a major booking site (such as Booking. com) and determine the percentage of fully booked hotels. For example, Booking.com will display the number of available hotels immediately after a search query is run.

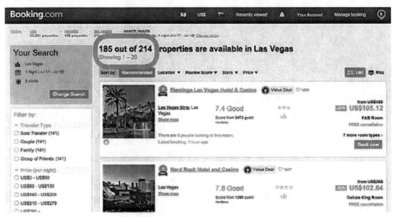

You can also find seasonal information from local tourist boards. They can give you an idea of hotel price fluctuations and crowd drawing events.

Make sure to adjust the prices for special dates well in advance, usually a year before the event takes place. For high traffic conferences or popular events, people tend to make bookings quite early.

Weekdays and weekends

Another facet to consider is whether your area is at its busiest during the week or the weekend. Business districts are usually highly sought Monday through Friday, whereas posh neighborhoods or regions that are replete with nightlife options are typically most popular on the weekends. Consider the genre of your neighborhood and adjust your prices accordingly. My area, for example, is very popular amongst young tourists, so I tend to set my weekend rates 25 - 30% above my weekday rates.

DO THIS NOW

Use Google to find out what conferences, events, and festivals your city hosts. Check the website of the main conference hosting associations in your area. Big sporting events can draw large crowds as well.

Weekly/monthly pricing

Airbnb gives you the option to set weekly/monthly pricing. You can use this setting to give automatic discounts for stays stretching longer than a week. I recommend offering a weekly price at about a 10 - 15% discount because you will save money due to: (1) less frequent cleanings, (2) lower general management costs, and (3) reduced liability from having a lower volume of guests.

There are two options for setting a weekly price: (1) general price and (2) custom price. I recommend using the custom price option so that you can still factor in high seasons and special events. If you don't, Airbnb will set all weeks to the same standard weekly price regardless of demand.

Most significant digit pricing

Did you ever notice that most products and services are sold at $9.99, $59.99, $499.99, and so on? If you're like me, you're probably aggravated to receive a penny back from a simple transaction. But before you condemn this seemingly silly practice, listen up. There is a method to the corporate world's madness.

This method is called "Most Significant Digit Pricing." Numerous studies have shown that sales will be significantly stronger for a product if it is listed at $29.99 versus $30. This is because human beings tend to focus on the most significant digit of a price. This is the first digit from left to right. In the previous example of $29.99, consumers would focus on the 2 and assess the value accordingly. That means that a product is more likely to be purchased at $29.99 versus $30. Since almost all people operate according to this principle, I suggest you adapt your pricing strategy to take advantage of this behavioral quirk.

Discounts

In my experience, guests frequently ask for discounts. When this happens, you will enter into a phase of negotiation. There are many excellent books written on this subject, the most notable being *Getting to Yes*, so I won't go into great detail here. Negotiation is a complex art and science, and I suggest you take the time to flip through a helpful book on the topic. That being said, I will summarize a few of the basic concepts.

Negotiation position

When negotiating, the most important factor is your negotiating position (or leverage). A negotiating position is determined by: (1) what you have to offer, (2) what you are willing to accept in return, and (3) what substitutes exist in the marketplace. Since this is an Airbnb rental, what you have to offer is your space. The minimum you are willing to accept is your lower bound, which is defined by your marginal costs plus a variable premium. The key question here is: what substitutes are out there?

Substitutes

The likelihood that you will secure a satisfying price will depend on the available substitutes.

Your guests' available substitutes are comprised of similar listings available during the same time frame. These listings likely reside in your neighborhood since most guests choose accommodations primarily based on location. Therefore, to get a feel for your competition, you can query the alternatives by performing a cursory search on Airbnb within your neighborhood. Fill in the dates requested and see what pops up.

Factors to consider when negotiating

There are a few important criteria to consider when contemplating a discount. You need to look at your calendar, the length of the stay requested, and the types of guests you plan to host. By carefully looking at these factors, you will be able to adeptly discern a reasonable point of compromise.

How well do the dates fit your calendar?

Let's say my calendar looks like this:

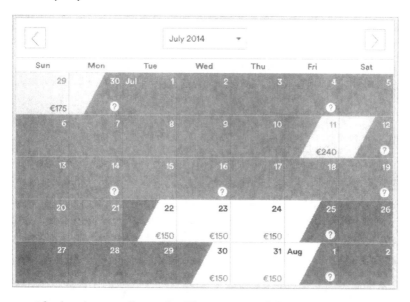

If a booking will neatly fill in a gap of days, I will be much more interested in reaching a negotiation. Why? Because a time frame that evenly eats up open space will make me significantly more money. For example, let's say I'm renting out my apartment for $200 per night. A potential guest sends me a message regarding a stay from May 2 to May 7. According to my calendar, this stay will slide nicely in between two previously established visits. But, this guest has requested a $40 per night discount. That means that instead of charging the full $1,000, I will only receive $800. Do I take it? In this case, I certainly would.

This is a great deal for me because most guests would likely only want to book my place for the weekend from May 2nd to May 5th. A weekend booking would leave the following Monday and Tuesday open, and since these days are typically difficult to fill, I risk losing $400. As such, agreeing to the discount will likely mean that I come out $200 ahead.

What is the length of the stay?

I employ a price system that provides guests with an automatic discount when they stay for six days. This is the optimal length for me with respect to profit and reviews. Accordingly, trip lengths that hover around six days are usually more likely to get a discount than short stays such as two or three nights.

What types of guests are coming?

My apartment in Amsterdam is located in an area of the city that has a lot of bars and nightclubs. As you would expect, I get tons of requests from young partygoers who want to rage for a long weekend. While I certainly cater to many of these folks, my ideal guests are retired couples seeking a quiet weekend. Why? They have a substantially lower liability level. I don't have to worry about elderly couples making loads of noise, inviting tons of friends over, drinking incessantly, inadvertently damaging my property while inebriated, and so on. Don't get me wrong, I too enjoy knocking back a few beers every now and then, but my point is that a well-mannered and calm couple is more economically deserving of a discount from me than a bustling group of 19-year olds.

Negotiating with your guests

As a rule of thumb, it is generally better to have your potential guests make the first offer. By allowing them to give you an initial price, you can get a feel for precisely how much they want to spend. Moreover, it enables you to offer a solid counter-offer, which will hopefully rein in an agreeable rate.

Whatever your position is, your aim should be to give your customer the impression that you're not eager to accept a discount. It maintains the notion that your apartment is a high value commodity with steady levels of demand. I have used this strategy with great success throughout my Airbnb career.

For example, let's say you're asking for $1,000 and your guests offer $800. In this case, I suggest counteroffering with $950. If, however, your potential guests stick firmly to their offer and are unwilling to meet in the middle, use the factors discussed above to decide whether or not you will accept their offer.

Extra charges

Airbnb gives you the option to charge for extras such as: (1) cleaning costs, (2) additional guests, and (3) a security deposit. Different hosts charge varying amounts, and you should tailor your charges according to the type of space you have as well as your experience level on Airbnb.

Charging for cleaning

Hosts are free to levy an additional fee for cleaning. I have found that applying such a charge does not negatively impact bookings. Accordingly, it makes sense to have a fixed cost for cleaning. A typical cleaning fee will range from $25 to $100 depending on the size of the apartment.

For your reference, I have compiled a list of 20 popular spaces across the globe and their respective cleaning fees.

CITY	CLEANING FEE (US $)	ROOMS
Amsterdam	$71.00	2 BR, 2BA
Amsterdam	$36.00	1 BR, 1 BA
Amsterdam	$43.00	1 BR, 1 BA
Amsterdam	$85.00	3 BR, 2 BA
London	$102.00	2 BR, 1 BA
London	$43.00	1 BR, 2 BA
London	$17.00	1 BR, 1 BA
London	$51.00	1 BR, 1 BA
Paris	$128.00	2 BR, 1 BA
Paris	$28.00	1 BR, 1 BA
Paris	$43.00	1 BR, 1 BA
Paris	$107.00	2 BR, 1.5 BA
New York	$75.00	1 BR, 1 BA
New York	$50.00	1 BR, 1 BA
New York	$75.00	1 BR, 1 BA
New York	$60.00	1 BR, 1.5 BA
Los Angeles	$120.00	2 BR, 2 BA
Los Angeles	$10.00	1 BR, 1 BA
Los Angeles	$15.00	1 BR, 1 BA
Los Angeles	$20.70	1 BR, 1.5 BA

For new listings, I recommend implementing a low fee. Why? Because cleaning fees are displayed on a per night basis. Translation: the more nights your guests book, the lower the cleaning fee will appear. Since new listings benefit most by hosting an abundance of short stays to build up reviews, a low fee is optimal. High fees might discourage potential guests from booking short stays.

Charging for additional guests

Adding on additional guests to a reservation will inherently increase your marginal costs. More people in your pad means more people using electricity, water, and gas. Additionally the greater the number of guests you host, the higher the liability is for damage to your property.

Personally, I charge a flat rate for the first four guests and add $25 for each extra guest thereafter. This is a fair rate that is on par with most other top listings in European cities.

Requesting a security deposit

Just like a standard landlord in a major city, you have the option to collect a security deposit for any damages or losses incurred during your guests' stay. You then have 48 hours after checkout to make a claim. Once you make a claim, your guests can either: (1) accept the claim and agree to payment or (2) refuse the claim and invoke Airbnb's mediation process.

Personally, I don't use a security deposit and I don't recommend it to others. There are a few reasons behind my rationale. Firstly, it could deter well-intentioned and responsible guests. I have several friends who are wary of security deposits because they've dealt with landlords in the past who falsely claimed damages. Truth be told, Airbnb is quite good at sniffing out the deceptive landlords, but still, guests certainly don't want to deal with this potential problem. Secondly, I've never had any damages other than extremely minor issues that can't be claimed. Lastly, in the case of real damages, you can always lean on the Airbnb Host Guarantee.

Beyond Pricing

When pricing is handled correctly, you can drastically augment your Airbnb profitability. Unfortunately, finding a solid base price and keeping on top of demand fluctuations can be a time consuming endeavor. If you don't have the time, patience, or data to proactively manage your pricing, I have good news for you.

Heeding the needs of the public, a sleek new start-up has entered the world of Airbnb hosting to solve the pricing conundrum once and for all. This innovative company goes by the name of Beyond Pricing. According to their mission statement, Beyond Pricing believes that "vacation owners should be able to tap into the same data that airlines, hotels, and other travel industries use to determine pricing. We view this as a democratization of data that you can use to power your listings' performance."

Beyond Pricing calculates the optimal rental price for your home based on the following criteria:

- Historic performance of your listing
- Performance of nearby listings
- Daily demand (based on hotel prices, flight data, and conferences/events)

Airbnb allows hosts to directly link their Airbnb listings to the Beyond Pricing service. The complex algorithms run every day, constantly recalculating the optimal price point. The Beyond Pricing service not only fine-tunes your price, but it automatically updates your calendar as well, substantially reducing the amount of work you need to do as a host. This means that you won't have to worry about setting prices, and can focus the bulk of your attention on what is most important: taking care of your guests.

Currently, Beyond Pricing offers the first two months of service for free. Once this trial period expires, the cost is $9 per month. The service is currently available in the following cities:

- Austin
- Boston
- Chicago
- Los Angeles
- Miami
- New York
- San Francisco
- Seattle

Soon, Beyond Pricing will be available in the following cities: London, Madrid, Barcelona, Rome, Amsterdam, and Tokyo. By 2015, the service is slated to go live worldwide. If you are interested in using this high caliber service, click Beyond Pricing to sign up today. Following the aforementioned link will get you an additional month of free membership.

Anna's Story

Before learning about Airbnb, I never rented out my house. I lived quite a normal life for a young professional in a major city. I woke up, ate breakfast, worked all day, came home to watch some TV, and went to sleep around 10 pm. For most people, this is a wonderful and easy routine, but it simply wasn't my cup of tea.

When I stumbled across Airbnb, I was intrigued. I saw people with all different types of houses renting out rooms to visitors from across the globe. I was a little hesitant at first because, being a woman, I was worried about inviting strangers into my home. But after I did a little homework, I realized that Airbnb is a widely used tool with a terrific track record.

Since I began using Airbnb to rent out my house, my life has changed a lot. First of all, I realized that I could be financially stable from Airbnb alone. That revelation prompted me to quit my boring job!

The financial freedom I enjoy has provided me with loads of time to spend in whatever way I choose. Since my ultimate passion is traveling, I take a lot of trips across Europe and Asia. I have been able to visit old friends and make new friends at an amazing rate. I feel truly blessed.

I also use my extra time to develop various business ideas. I hope I will one day achieve entrepreneurial success, but in the meantime, I'm quite happy earning a steady bit of income from my house!

Even if I had the option to switch over to long-term rentals, I would never do it. First of all, people looking for short-stays are generally very happy and friendly since they are on holiday. This always creates a good vibe from the start. Also I love showing my guests around the city, taking them out to nice restaurants, and introducing them to cool tourist attractions. They really appreciate my effort, and that makes me feel terrific!

I have also found that being a good host is wonderfully rewarding, and I have discovered a passion for helping people. I love making my guests feel good because it makes me feel good too. I will definitely be a life long user of Airbnb and highly recommend it to everyone.

CHAPTER 4

Your Guests

"There is only one boss. The customer.
And he can fire everybody in the company from the
chairman on down, simply by sending his money
somewhere else."

- Sam Walton, Founder of Walmart and Sam's Club

The customer reigns supreme. The customer is in charge of everything. The customer dictates whether or not your business makes a profit, expands to new territories, or shuts its doors forever. As a host, your guests are your customers, and they are the most important aspect of your accommodations business. You should constantly strive to make your guests' experience the best it can be.

If you are out of town when your guests arrive, you will probably never have a chance to meet them face-to-face. But, all is not lost. You can still do a lot to improve your guests' experience remotely by communicating with them via email and text message.

Needless to say, things don't always go as planned. Your guests will inevitably encounter problems at some point. At one time or another, my Internet has been down, my TV has stopped working, or my manager has missed a check-in due to a miscommunication. These unpredictable issues can result in deep perturbation. There are ways, however, that you can mitigate the damage. The extent to which these mishaps will negatively affect your business depends largely on how you handle the situation, not the situation itself.

Finally, it is imperative that you recognize the inherent value of your guests. Not only do they provide you with money and a potential review, but they also serve as live and present sources of feedback. No matter how well you prepare your house, you will miss something. Lucky for you, chances are that your guests will eventually identify whatever deficiencies exist. Requesting feedback from your guests allows you to harness this input and expeditiously make needed improvements.

Communicating with your guests

One reason why a lot of visitors prefer short-stay accommodations is because of the personal attention and communication. If you communicate well with your guests, you can significantly improve their experience before they set a foot inside your place.

Pre-booking

Potential guests can contact you in two ways. They can make an *inquiry* through the "Contact Host" button, or they can send you a *booking request* by clicking on the red "Request to Book" button.

€149   Per Night ▼

Check In   Check Out   Guests

mm/dd/yyyy   mm/dd/yyyy   1 ▼

Request to Book

Inquiries

When you start receiving messages from potential customers, remember to always be ultra responsive. Being reachable and responsive is one of the central keys to stellar customer service. After all if people can't get a hold of you, it doesn't matter how amazing your product and website are. Moreover, with the development of mobile technology, the general public is growing more and more impatient. The demand for quick turnarounds and instant access to customer service is only growing.

So as soon as you get an inquiry, respond. Here is a good rule of thumb: as long as you're awake, get back to any and every inquiry *within one hour*. You can set up a special alert on your email so that you get a notification right when an inquiry is sent. I follow the same one-hour rule as a businessman, and both internal and external clients rave about my excellent service. Guests will undoubtedly appreciate the extra effort.

A short response time is also highly beneficial because most users contact multiple hosts at once. By being the first one to respond, you greatly increase the likelihood of a booking.

Most inquiries are short messages that read something like:

> Hi Jasper,
>
> Is your apartment available for our travel dates (May 15 - May 20)?
>
> Thanks, John.

My standard response is as follows:

> Dear John,
>
> Thank you so much for your inquiry. I'm happy to let you know that my place is available for your dates and that you are more than welcome to stay there. I'm sure you'll enjoy my comfortable apartment and the amazing neighborhood.
>
> If you have any questions, please feel free to ask. I'm here to help and I will do my best to make your stay as comfortable as possible. After you make the booking, I will send you an extensive guide to both my apartment and the neighborhood.
>
> I'm looking forward to hosting you!
>
> Best regards, Jasper

Sometimes an inquiry contains specific questions:

> Hi Jasper,
>
> Your apartment looks terrific, though I have a few questions. Is there any available parking? Are the stairs very steep? Is there a hair dryer in the house?
>
> Thanks, John

Part of being responsive is sending a fully comprehensive email. If your guests ask you a set of questions, you need to answer everything in a clear and organized manner. If they don't get all the responses they need to make an informed decision, you could lose out to a competing host who delivers the requisite information. A good response to the above inquiry should look like this:

Dear John,

Thank you so much for your inquiry. I'm happy to answer all of your questions.

• **Is there any available parking?** - There is no parking within my building, but there is an excellent parking structure approximately 90 feet from my front door. They charge $10 per day if you simply leave your car there. But if you'd like to come and go, you can pay $15 per day.

• **Are the stairs very steep?** - The stairs are a bit steeper than normal stairs, but I can assure you that I've never had a guest slip and fall. Moreover, I have hosted children and older couples, and neither group has ever had any issues with the staircase.

• **Is there a hair dryer in the house?** - Absolutely. There is a very nice hairdryer in the top-level bathroom.

If you have any additional questions, please feel free to ask. Thank you, and I am looking forward to hosting you!

Best regards, Jasper

You want to present the information requested in the simplest format possible. Make the data visually clear and keep your responses concise yet detailed enough to quench any lingering or subsequent questions. The goal is to provide them with a one-stop shop of information so they can make an instantaneous booking.

A quick piece of forward thinking advice: look at any questions within an inquiry as an indication of a lack of information in your listing. Try to incorporate the details you provide into your general listing whenever feasible.

Booking requests

When you receive a booking request, you have 24 hours to respond. But once again, I recommend responding within one hour. A delayed response can cost you a booking and a positive review, both severe losses.

If you will be traveling or working abroad and your Internet access might be spotty, consider hiring a temporary assistant or intern to manage your bookings. Make sure that they adhere to the same responsiveness strictures.

If you can't find anyone to assume this role, you have the option to "hide" your listing temporarily. While you may miss out on some bookings, your position in the search results won't be compromised by a subpar response time and response percentage.

Finally, make sure to check your "Never Responded" inbox periodically to ensure that you haven't missed any messages.

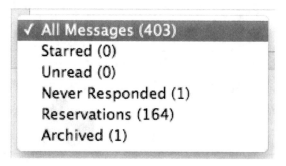

Inquiries to transact outside of Airbnb

Sometimes guests will ask you if they can pay you cash on arrival instead of going through the Airbnb system. This tactic is sometimes appealing to guests as the 6-12% booking fee is avoided. It may also be appealing to a host because it negates the 3% service fee that Airbnb charges all hosts.

Although it might sound enticing to pocket a pile of cash and avoid a set of fees, I firmly advise against this strategy for a few reasons. First of all, I simply believe that it's morally wrong to use a service and not pay for it. Were it not for Airbnb, the afore-mentioned transaction would never have been possible. Airb-nb provides an integral service; they should be aptly rewarded. Secondly, bucking the system will only harm the platform. The aggregate effect of this type of behavior could spell disaster for Airbnb, and that will negatively impact their user base… which, of course, is you.

Thirdly, accepting cash under the table is against Airbnb's policies. By listing your space on their website, you implicitly accept the terms and conditions that prohibit this behavior. If you violate these rules, you risk being banned indefinitely from Airbnb.

Finally, there are a lot of benefits that come with booking through the Airbnb system:

- You are protected by the Airbnb Host Guarantee

- You can receive a review from your guests

- You are protected against last minute cancellations (de-pending on your cancellation policy)

- Airbnb will help you resolve any issues or disputes should they arise

- Your guests are more likely to respect your property and rules because of your ability to leave them a review

In sum, don't transact outside Airbnb. It's just not worth it.

Post-booking

The moment I confirm a booking, I send my customers the following message:

Dear John,

Thank you for your booking! I'm looking forward to hosting you and I'm sure you will have an unforgettable time in Amsterdam.

I will send you all the information you need to ensure a perfect stay, including:

• Details on how to get to my apartment

• Instructions on how to use the electronics and appliances

• A local guide with plenty of insider recommendations for hot spots in my neighborhood. In the meantime if you have any questions, please don't hesitate to contact me. The best way to reach me is by email (email address) or by phone (phone number).

Lastly, if you have already made travel arrangements, please let me know your: (1) arrival time and (2) local means of transport. For example, if you plan to arrive by plane, please include your airline and flight number. This will enable me to prepare a timely and proper welcome! Safe travels.

Best regards, Jasper

Shortly after I send the above email, I follow up by shooting over a set of detailed directions as well as a copy of my guidebook. This level of care lays the foundation for an impeccable review by making your new guests feel welcomed before they set foot in your city!

About a week before my guests arrive, I contact them again to confirm the arrival date and time. I also ask if they will need any assistance bringing their luggage inside of the apartment.

I strongly encourage you to follow these customer care guidelines. It will help differentiate you from the masses and make your guests feel extra special. It's a win-win situation: you expend a minimal amount of effort at no additional cost, and your guests feel substantially more welcomed and comfortable. In the event that a problem does arise during the stay, this level of service will make your guests feel far less inclined to leave a negative review.

Reaching out to guests during their stay

Customer service doesn't end once the guests have arrived. It is your duty to keep up with your guests throughout the entirety of their stay. After the guests have checked-in, confirm that everything is satisfactory. Also, encourage them to keep you abreast of any issues or concerns. You can only remedy issues that you are aware of. Here is a letter that I send out to my guests mid stay:

Dear John,

I'm glad that you have made it safely to my humble abode! I hope you enjoy my apartment and my awesome hometown of Amsterdam.

Please do not hesitate to contact me throughout your stay. If you have any questions/concerns/comments at absolutely anytime, please shoot me an email (email address) or give me a call (phone number). I want your stay to be absolutely terrific, and will work with you to ensure an excellent visit.

Take care and enjoy your holiday!

Best regards, Jasper

Sending a post stay thank-you

After your guests have left, follow up with a final message:

Dear John,

I hope you thoroughly enjoyed your stay at my apartment in Amsterdam! Thanks for being a great guest and treating my apartment with respect.

As I'm always striving to improve my guest's experience, please let me know if you have any feedback or suggestions.

If you have enjoyed your stay, please share your story by writing a quick review on Airbnb. This helps future guests make a more informed decision about my apartment. I would truly appreciate this!

Finally, I've written a review for you as well. Since you were a terrific guest, I wrote a very positive one. This will help you get accepted to subsequent bookings in the future.

I wish you all the best, and you are always welcome to come back and stay at my apartment again!

Best regards, Jasper

Notice how I *specifically ask for feedback*. I do this because happy guests are statistically less inclined to leave feedback. Studies show that happy customers usually share their experience with 5 individuals, whereas unhappy guests naturally broadcast their disappointment with 10 individuals. Since I'm after good reviews, I encourage my pleased customers to write me a review. Otherwise, the pleasant stay will go unreported and my reputation does not benefit. Additionally, prompting my guest for feedback is an excellent way of learning about minor imperfections in my apartment that could be improved.

Problems with your guests

Even if you are the perfect host, the utter embodiment of a five-star concierge/bellman/tour guide, problems will arise. It's a reality in any business. When something goes wrong, remember to keep your cool. Take a deep breath, breathe into your abdomen, and close your eyes. It's damage control time. The last thing you want is a bad review for your listing; therefore, make a battle plan to calm your guests and mitigate the damage.

Broken or damaged items

No matter how new or technologically advanced your appliances are, things will eventually break down and stop working. Light bulbs, microwaves, vacuum cleaners, and other household items will all meet their demise one day. When something stops working, don't jump to blame your guests. Consider the damage done and honestly ascertain whether or not it is beyond the scope of normal wear and tear. Only when it's absolutely clear that something has been damaged by irresponsible or careless behavior should you bring it up. You must recognize that any attempt to recoup a loss from your guests is review suicide. In other words, you might win the battle, but you'll lose the war. Accordingly, I suggest you do it sparingly and only when necessary.

If you have indeed determined that a guest has wrongfully damaged your property, you can ask to be reimbursed. If a disagreement arises and your guest refuses to make restitution, you can ask Airbnb to mediate. Airbnb will collect an account of the events from both parties and then make a ruling based on their analysis. From my experience, the Airbnb mediation process is extremely fair and prompt.

Unhappy guests

The magnitude of unhappiness will vary wildly from guest to guest. Some disdained patrons will gently bring to your attention minor problems, whereas others might be so displeased with the interior of your place that they will literally leave after check-in. Depending on the situation and the guest, you may or may not be able to fix the problem and pacify the guest. If not, you can still salvage your reputation if you handle the situation properly.

Fixable problems

Whenever a problem arises, your first course of action is to determine if it is a fixable issue. If it is, fix it. Some examples that I have encountered are as follows:

- **No toaster** – One group of friendly guests were quite disappointed that they couldn't toast their bread in the morning. Toast was a staple component of this family's breakfast diet, and they were keen enough on having a morning piece of toast to contact me about the missing appliance. Since I wanted to make them extra happy, and the price of a toaster was fairly low, I had my cleaning lady buy one for them the same day. I solved the problem, made my customers happy, and stocked my apartment with an appliance that would benefit future guests.

- **Broken Xbox** – Back in September of 2012, I hosted an entourage of four college guys. In addition to exploring the city, they wanted to engage in a friendly video game tournament. Unfortunately for them and unbeknownst to me, my Xbox was no longer working. As soon as they let me know, I called the local electronics store and had them deliver a new Xbox to my apartment. My faulty Xbox was replaced and I received an absolutely stellar review.

- **Cold bedroom** – When a couple chose my apartment for a romantic getaway, they were quite upset when one of the radiators in my house didn't heat up, causing the bedroom to be frigid. What did I do? I immediately hired someone to fix it, and the remainder of their stay was as toasty as could be.

Do you notice the central theme amongst these stories? If there is a fixable issue, I fix it right away. Problems that can be solved usually don't cause guests to be unhappy *if you solve them as soon as possible*. As long as you react appropriately and promptly, you won't be blamed. In fact, if you respond right away, you may receive a better review than if nothing had gone wrong in the first place!

Unfixable problems

In some instances, problems simply can't be fixed. This is either because the problem isn't solvable on short notice, or it has an external cause that you simply can't address (such as a downed server, a noisy neighbor, etc).

When an insurmountable challenge like this arises, here's what you do:

1. **Apologize vehemently to your guests for the inconvenience** – Even if the problem has nothing to do with you or your apartment, offer your condolences regardless.

2. **Cover any extra costs incurred** – If your guests are forced to buy earplugs to blot out the noise from a nearby party, offer to pay for the added expenses.

3. **Offer a partial refund** – Determining how much money to give back is a highly nuanced question and will depend greatly on a number of variables. Nevertheless, I suggest trying to overcompensate. Even if the visit amounts to a short-term loss, you can hopefully squeeze out a positive review (or at least avoid a negative review).

You might think these suggestions are over the top, but in the long-term, they are the best routes to optimize your listing. First of all, unfixable problems like this rarely occur. Handling them aggressively and proactively will barely affect your revenue stream. Secondly, taking drastic action greatly reduces the chance of a bad review. Finally, with respect to the partial refund, my guests usually don't take me up on this offer and simply thank me for the gesture.

Here are some examples from my experience as a host:

-   **Unclean apartment upon check-in** – When I hosted a group of two couples from the U.S., I had a miscommunication with my cleaning lady regarding a cleaning appointment. Consequently, my apartment wasn't clean before the guests arrived. Needless to say, they were quite furious. My cleaning lady came later in the day to clean the place, but the damage had already been done. As a peace offering, I offered a partial refund. My guests happily accepted the money and didn't leave me with a bad review.

- **Broken washer and dryer** – One reason why my apartment is such a draw to tourists is because it has an in-unit washer and dryer, a rare luxury in my neighborhood. During a particular guest's visit, my washing machine broke down. I called several repair shops, but despite my best effort, I couldn't replace it in time. Because he absolutely needed to do his laundry, my guest was forced to go to a nearby laundromat. I apologized profusely and offered to: (1) pay for his laundry and (2) give him a partial refund. My guest thanked me, but then told me not to worry about the expenses. Despite the major inconvenience, he didn't leave me a bad review.

- **Late night lockout** – I once hosted a bubbly group of Australian college students on holiday. They were excited about the nightlife options in my neighborhood, and took every opportunity available to explore the restaurants and bars. On one of those fateful nights, they came back to my place a bit inebriated and completely unable to unlock the door. It was very late and they couldn't get me or my cleaning lady on the phone. As a result, they were forced to check into a nearby hotel. The next day, I headed over to the apartment to let them in. To my surprise, there was no problem with the lock or the keys; my guests were simply unable to apply the proper force to the turnkey. Even though the lock was functional, I offered to compensate my guests for the cost of the hotel. They ended up taking half of my offer. When it was time to leave a review, they gave me five stars in every category and a terrific write-up!

Handling guests who want to leave

Even if your apartment is pristine and well organized, you might encounter a guest who thinks your apartment is unacceptable. When this happens, you will have few options to consider. I suggest offering a refund with the condition that the unhappy guest refrains from writing a review. You are free to charge the guest, but I would weigh the value of the money against the damage of a negative review. Since these occurrences will be far and few between, the best course of action is to preserve your reputation and protect your future profits.

Issuing a refund

There are two ways to give your guests a refund. Firstly, in the event that a guest cancels his reservation prior to check-in, you can use Airbnb's "Issue Refund" button. This enables you to return any cash above and beyond what is normally given according to your particular cancellation policy. Your 3% host fee will be adjusted to the final amount you charge.

For all other refunds, you can use Airbnb's "Resolutions Tool" (which can be found in the "Resolution Center"). All you have to do is choose the appropriate reservation, enter the desired amount and currency, and draft a short message to your guest. Bear in mind that all refunds are final, and the tool can only be used for reservations in the last 30 days.

Feedback from guests

Getting feedback from your guests will be vital to your success. Adjusting your listing based on real-time feedback is the best way to augment guest satisfaction. There are several ways to get feedback from your guests.

Reviews

After guests have stayed at your place, they have the option to leave a review. Hopefully your reviews will be chock-full of glowing praise and appreciation. If, however, you find yourself getting some honest and sincere pieces of constructive criticism, take them to heart. Without feedback, you would be unable to intelligently improve your space. The lesson here is this: instead of letting a rough review upset you, look at it as a positive opportunity to make a needed improvement.

Private feedback

Airbnb offers guests the option to leave private feedback. These personal messages will only be visible to the host. Guests often feel more comfortable mentioning small issues here than in the reviews so that your reputation is not affected negatively. If you are interested in proactively pushing your guests to make suggestions, I recommend asking them to submit feedback via a private message.

Asking guests for feedback

After your guests have left, encourage them to provide feedback in your post stay thank-you message. Emphasize the fact that you would appreciate even minor feedback since you constantly strive to increase your guests' satisfaction.

Taking feedback seriously

Feedback is terrific, but without accompanied action, it is useless. The point of hearing the thoughts and concerns of your guests is so that you make necessary improvements. It is important to put your ego aside when dealing with customer feedback. Even if you think that your apartment is wonderful, there is always room for improvement. Moreover, different perspectives and personalities can have vastly different standards. Try not to look at suggestions through your own personal lens.

Accepting bookings

The number one question I get asked is this: "aren't you worried that a bunch of strangers might completely trash your apartment?" To be completely honest, I'm not worried in the slightest. There are a number of reasons why, and the next sections will parse them.

Choosing your guests

Airbnb allows hosts to accept and deny bookings on a completely independent and subjective basis. There is no explicit punishment for rejecting a booking. It is important to note, however, that rejecting bookings on a routine basis will affect your "Acceptance Rate." This is one of the metrics considered by Airbnb when calculating your search rank. Accordingly, I suggest you use this option when necessary, but employ it sparingly.

Personally, I prefer renting to older couples or entire families. I usually find that both types of travelers are a bit more tame and predictable. The caveat to this preference is the majority of my guests happen to be young party fanatics. That is fine, and I am open to hosting any genre of guest, but I just make sure to conduct proper due diligence when I get an inquiry from a group of ravenous Londoners with a penchant for clubbing and late night snacks.

The quickest and easiest way to check out potential guests is to view their profiles. You can also take a glimpse at their verifications and reviews.

Your Current Verifications

Email Address

You have confirmed your email: jasperairbnb@gmail.com. A confirmed email is important to allow us to securely communicate with you.

Phone Number

Rest assured, your number is only shared with another Airbnb member once you have a confirmed booking.

Facebook

Sign in with Facebook and discover your trusted connections to hosts and guests all over the world.

[Disconnect]   ❷

Google

Connect your Airbnb account to your Google account for simplicity and ease.

[Disconnect]   ❷

LinkedIn

Create a link to your professional life by connecting your Airbnb and LinkedIn accounts.

[Disconnect]   ❷

If potential guests don't have any reviews, it doesn't necessarily mean that they aren't trustworthy. They could be awesome and responsible adults who are simply brand new to Airbnb. If you want to consider a newbie, the onus is on you to dig a little deeper. For example, you can use the "Discuss" option to begin a conversation with the potential guest. Feel free to ask any pertinent questions, such as: (1) why are you visiting my city, (2) how many people are you traveling with, (3) what are you hoping to do/see, and (4) what types of activities do you like to partake in during your free time.

Instant Book restrictions

Airbnb offers hosts the option of enabling an "Instant Book" feature. This gives potential guests the option of making an instantaneous reservation. This means that guests do not have wait for host approval; the booking is finalized as soon as the "Instant Book" button is clicked.

If you choose to utilize the "Instant Book" feature, there are still two ways to filter applicants. Firstly, you can require that guests have "positive reviews." Secondly, you can specify an advanced notice period in order for the "Instant Book" option to be available. The options for advanced notice include 1 day, 3 days, and 7 days.

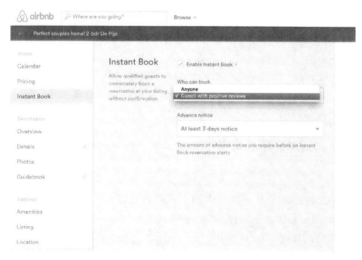

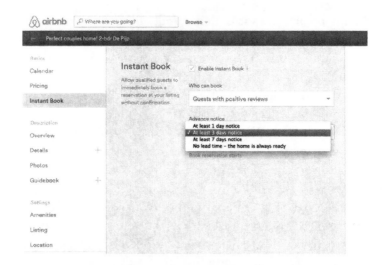

Airbnb Host Guarantee

The Airbnb Host Guarantee covers you up to $1,000,000 against theft or vandalism by your guests. Enough said.

Most people are good people

As a long time Airbnb host, my experience indicates that most guests will respect your space totally and completely. Translation: people are, for the most part, inherently good. My usage of the site has been very positive and I've never had any serious problems. The bottom line is this: don't let your apprehension of the unknown stifle a terrific moneymaking opportunity.

Interacting with guests renting single rooms

If you are only renting out a single room in your household, you will most likely be sharing the common areas with your guests. This has certain advantages over an entire space. Firstly, you have more time to build a personal relationship with your guests. In addition, you will be in close proximity, making it much easier to answer questions and offer advice. You could even pamper your temporary resident with a few home cooked meals. I recommend preparing breakfast, as it is a universally liked selection of dishes that are fairly easy to make.

Be sure to communicate clearly with your guests so that their expectations are accurately tempered. For example, let them know up front whether you will have friends over, if you have noise regulations that kick in at certain times, or if you will be around for the duration of the stay. This will prevent potential annoyances and problems.

While it is a great idea to try and build a connection with your guests, be mindful of the nature of the relationship you develop. Try to read your guests and behave accordingly. For example, some guests might not be looking to get to close with anyone during their visit. For introverted folks who prefer to spend time by themselves, an overly friendly host can be an unwanted nuisance. Also, respect the privacy of your guests. Always knock before entering their rooms, and remember to cover yourself up around the house.

Jordan's Story

In 2012, I decided to make the move from Washington, D.C. to Los Angeles, California. My family had relocated to the west coast, and I thought it was a good idea for all of us to be together. Plus, Los Angeles is known for beautiful weather and fantastic nightlife: two added perks that made my decision an easy one.

When I arrived in L.A., I was pleasantly surprised by the cost of apartments. Compared to D.C., real estate was significantly cheaper. As a result, I was able to afford a two-bedroom apartment by myself. I figured that I would use the extra space as an office for my entrepreneurial projects, or if need be, a guest bedroom for my out of town friends.

One Sunday afternoon, I was watching football with a couple of my D.C. buddies at a sports bar. A friend of mine introduced me to a guy named Julian, who was in town for a week or so. Julian was a drifter of sorts. He had no permanent address, and spent all of his time traveling the world. As we eased into a conversation, he began talking about Airbnb. He told me how he used it when he traveled, and that he no longer stayed in hotels or hostels. The concept was intriguing. It sounded like a terrific and affordable way to see the world. As soon as I got home, I began reading about it voraciously. But I wasn't nearly as fascinated by the renting aspect as I was by the hosting. It quickly occurred to me that I was perfectly situated to make some supplemental income with my spare bedroom.

After reviewing a number of listings in my area, I created a profile with all the trimmings. I added a collection of nice photographs along with a fully loaded description. I was ready to launch my new business.

Since joining the site, I have been thrilled with the results. I have a number of requests each month to rent my private room. When I feel like having a guest, I accept the inquiry. When I don't, I don't. The supplemental income usually covers about half of my rent, and that's with an occupancy rate of less than 30%. If I wanted to crank it up, I could more than cover my rent each month. But the way I look at it, every bit of cash I get from Airbnb is a bonus. I don't push too hard to maximize the number of guests; I simply do what is comfortable and convenient for me.

A fringe benefit of this whole process is that I've met a bunch of interesting people. Because I get to choose who stays with me, I generally pick people who I think I will get along with. This has netted me friends across Europe, Asia, and South America. I'm currently in the process of planning several lengthy trips to visit my international guests. All in all, it has been a terrific experience with countless rewards.

CHAPTER 5

Reviews

"I think it's very important to have a feedback loop, where you're constantly thinking about what you've done and how you could be doing it better."

- Elon Musk, Co-founder of SpaceX

Reviews are the foundation of the service industry. Hotels, restaurants, personal trainers, physicians, real estate agents, tutors, and any other service-based profession must live and die by the review system. As the world has grown ever more interconnected, and social media has engulfed every aspect of our lives, the power of customer feedback has grown exponentially. Advertising and marketing are still vastly important tools, but at the end of the day, cyber word of mouth is fast becoming the ultimate determining factor for a business venture's success.

The Airbnb review system creates an opportunity for you as a host. But watch your step; if you are careless with your first wave of guests, you may be relegated to Airbnb mediocrity, or worse yet, failure. But, however, if you handle your first few customers with attention and care, you can fortify a solid reputation and a stable launch pad. Mastery of this facet will ensure your long-term success.

When you're starting out as a host, your number one goal should be securing as many positive reviews as possible. This will benefit you in three identifiable ways:

1. **Higher position in search results** – Airbnb uses the amount of reviews that you have as one of several factors in determining the ranking of your listing. As the number of positive reviews grows, you will slowly climb the ladder of search results for your city and neighborhood.

2. **More clicks from potential guests** – When a set of listings populates, users see the primary photo along with some other bits of information. One of the prominent pieces of data is the number of reviews written, which can be seen in the lower right corner above the price.

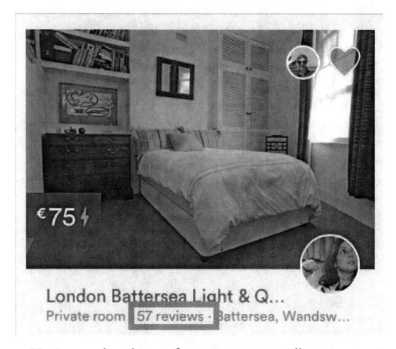

London Battersea Light & Q...
Private room 57 reviews · Battersea, Wandsw...

Having an abundance of positive reviews will encourage visitors to click on your listing to check it out. The reason behind this phenomenon is the concept of "social proof," the idea that universally liked products are usually high quality. Humans naturally gravitate towards goods and services that are popular. Alternatively, if you only have a few reviews, visitors might unfairly assume that your place is subpar.

3. **Higher conversion rate of inquiries to bookings** – Positive reviews will increase the number of viewers who actually make a booking with you. Again, the added level of trust inherently gained by a strong flow of positive reviews is often the added nudge that most guests need to sign the dotted line.

The Airbnb review system

An Airbnb review is comprised of two parts: (1) an "Overall Guest Satisfaction" rating based on a five-star system, which is divided into six subcategories; and (2) a written review that summarizes your guests' experience.

Overall Guest Satisfaction

The "Overall Guest Satisfaction" rating consists of six factors: (1) accuracy, (2) communication, (3) cleanliness, (4) location, (5) check-in, and (6) value.

Four of these factors are dynamic and within your control: accuracy, communication, cleanliness, and check-in. Your baseline standard in these categories should be five stars across the board. If you treat your guests well, they should always give you five stars. If not, you've likely done something wrong. Here is a quick overview of each of the categories along with some helpful tips on how to maximize their scores:

- **Accuracy** – This category is meant to be a reflection of the connection between your listing and your space. Were the photos proper depictions of the actual look and feel of the apartment? Were the available appliances and amenities in line with what was described? Is the proximity to fun nightspots accurate? Make sure that your listing is a truthful representation. Never promise anything that you can't deliver.

- **Communication** – You need to communicate with your guests before, during, and after their stay. Being responsive and available is a big part of this equation. For more details on stellar communication, flip back to the section Communicating with your guests.

- **Cleanliness** – Remember, five-star hotel cleanliness is the standard. Every inch of your space needs to be absolutely spotless. If you've had a subpar review in this category, make sure to ask your guests for specific feedback. Once you learn of the issue, remedy it immediately. For more details on keeping a clean apartment, flip back to the section Routine cleaning.

- **Check-in** – Check-ins are simple, yet a mismanaged one can blow the entire stay. Remember, newly arriving guests might have just completed a long and tiring journey. The last thing they want to deal with is an unnecessary wait outside of your apartment. For more details on ensuring a smooth check-in, flip back to the section Check-ins.

- **Location** - This rating is out of your control; you either have a terrific location or you don't. There are ways, however, that you can boost this rating without hiring a helicopter and a construction crew to airlift your apartment to the city center. For example, if you douse your guests with terrific information regarding transportation, restaurants, nightlife, and tourist attractions, your guests will be able to make the most out their visit despite the second-rate location. The best way to deliver this information is by writing a detailed and well-organized guidebook for your guests. For more details on creating a terrific guidebook, flip back to the section Creating a custom made guidebook.

- **Value** – Although this rating sounds fairly straightforward, it is quite tricky to understand. You might initially presume that your goal is to aim for five stars. However, that is not necessarily the optimal outcome. If you are netting five stars in this category and getting more than an 80% booking rate, you are likely charging too little for your place. If this is the case, you need to raise your price. I recommend knocking it up in 10% increments until you see the booking rate start to drop. Once you find the price sweet spot where bookings are still relatively strong, you will be maximizing your profits. Don't worry if your "value" rating drops a bit during this experimentation phase; it will barely affect your search result ranking, as you will likely only experience a slight dip.

Written reviews

The written review provides your guests with an opportunity to describe their experience in a highly personalized manner. This is their chance to speak to future guests in their own voice. Although the star rating is the first data point potential guests will look at, thorough consumers will often read through the written reviews to get a personalized glimpse of the listing. Accordingly, it is in your best interest to encourage former guests to offer a rating as well as a written review.

Getting positive reviews

I've worked hard to be the best host I can be. Thankfully, my guests have rewarded me for my efforts in the form of solid ratings and praiseful reviews. Since I travel 10 out of 12 months, I normally don't have the opportunity to welcome my guests personally. But, because I have carefully selected a solid manager, I have still been able to do exceedingly well.

At the end of the day, the best way to get a great review is to build a strong and sincere relationship with your guests. How do you go about doing this? In short, be an awesome host. If you have implemented all the advice from the previous chapters, you should be on your way to receiving solely positive reviews. Just to reiterate, there are a few key points that are essential to nailing a solid review.

Your space must be clean

As I've mentioned in the Routine cleaning section, your place has to be spotless. Don't try to economize on this. In fact, you should go the extra mile. Paying a premium for a good cleaner is most definitely worth it and should be considered an investment. As an added bonus, most people will be less inclined to make a mess or damage your apartment if it appears pristine.

Everything must work

Whatever amenities and appliances you mention on your listing must be in working order. Guests will arrive at your apartment with the expectation that everything you say is true. Accordingly, be on the lookout for any broken or missing items. Things to check regularly include:

- Heating
- Air conditioning

- Shower
- Kitchen appliances
- TV
- WiFi

Writing a nice review for your guests

As I've stated, a collection of solid reviews is the only sure fire way to a steady stream of guests. One of the best ways to ensure that your customers actually write you a pleasant review is to preemptively submit one for them.

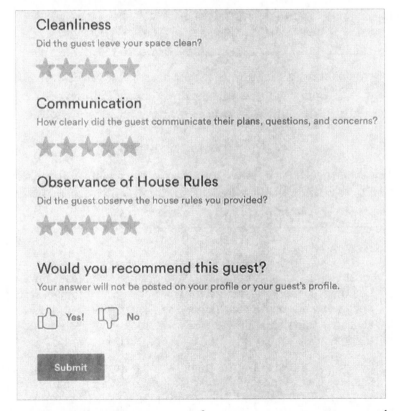

When submitting a review for your guests, you can provide feedback in three categories: (1) cleanliness, (2) communication, and (3) observance of house rules. As a general principle, I give all my guests five stars across the board unless I had a significant issue. I also vote "yes" for recommending your guests to other hosts. Finally, I draft a glowing written review. I usually submit my review immediately after checkout.

In addition, I typically send a private note to each of my guests. Here is an example of a private message:

Dear John,

Thanks for being a great guest! I hope you've enjoyed your stay at my apartment in Amsterdam. Please let me know if you ever want to come back in the future!

Best regards, Jasper

P.S. Since you were a terrific guest, I've gone ahead and left you a stellar review to help you with future bookings!

Make sure to mention that you have left a very positive review. This is especially important since guests will not be able to see a host review unless they have posted a review themselves.

Asking for a review

If a guest neglects to write you a review after your first request, I suggest waiting about one week to re-initiate with a follow-up message. My reminder message looks like this:

Dear John,

I just wanted to send you a friendly reminder to please leave a review for me. Reviews are the lifeblood of an Airbnb host, and I rely on them to maintain my reputation. Moreover, I'm always looking to improve my space, so any suggestions or feedback you might have would be greatly appreciated.

By the way, I've gone ahead and written a review for you! Since you were such a terrific guest, I gave you top marks in all available categories. I hope this helps you out for future reservations.

Thank you again!
Best Regards, Jasper

The option to leave a review expires 14 days after guests have checked out. If former guests haven't left a review after 12 days, I send one final message to try and motivate them. My final message looks like this:

> Dear John,
>
> I hope all is well with you. I just wanted to send a final reminder to please leave a review for me. Guests only have a 14-day window to leave a review after checkout, and we are fast approaching that deadline.
>
> If you have time to say a few kind words about your stay, I would be greatly appreciative.
>
> Thank you again!
>
> Best regards, Jasper

Bad reviews

Even if you are a super duper mega host with customer service expertise pouring out of every orifice, it will be almost impossible to please all of your guests. You will assuredly come across that one grumpy guest who encounters a few unavoidable problems during his stay and chooses to take out his frustration via a negative review. When the inevitable day arrives, you must make sure to address the review head on so as to minimize the damage done to your brand.

Taking them seriously

When you get a bad review, do not brush it off. Face the criticism head on. There is no such thing as an inapplicable complaint. There is almost always a reason behind a guest's displeasure or unhappiness. It is your job to accurately assess the complaint and discern what could be improved in the future. Don't let your ego get in the way of optimizing your space.

Leaving a reaction

Although you can't have a bad review expunged from your profile, you can leave a responsive reaction. Airbnb provides hosts with a two week window to leave a response. I recommend doing this for every negative review. This will provide future guests an opportunity to hear your side of the story when scanning the reviews. Now, when you write a response, don't be defensive. Instead, apologize for any unease and let your guests know that you are taking the complaint seriously. Moreover, state that you will remedy the issue immediately and that it will no longer be a problem. Finally, state within the response that you would love to host these guests again, and if they are willing, that you will offer them a discount. This good faith attempt to rectify whatever wrong transpired will show your viewers that you have every intention of providing stellar customer service.

Here's an example of a negative review:

> We were very disappointed with this apartment. The shower wasn't clean, there weren't enough towels, and we were woken up at night by loud noises coming from outside. We wouldn't stay here again.
>
> John

If I were responding to a complaint like this, I would address each and every concern raised. John has mentioned three in particular: (1) the cleanliness of the shower, (2) the number of towels, and (3) the noise level during the night. Additionally, I would apologize sincerely and invite the guest to come back at a discounted rate in the future. Here is what my response would look like:

Dear John,

I'm sorry to hear that your stay was subpar. As a host, I always strive for excellence, and I am truly disappointed that I was unable to meet your expectations. I am constantly looking for ways to improve my guest's experience, and I thank you for your feedback.

After reading your review, I met with my manager and my cleaner to rectify all the issues that you mentioned. In particular, the following changes have been made:

1. I instructed my cleaner to take special care of the shower

2. I have bought four extra bath towels

3. I have purchased a collection of disposable earplugs for my future guests.

I would love to have you re-visit my apartment to make up for your experience. If you choose to stay with me again, I would be happy to give you a 50% discount. Thank you, and once again, I truly apologize.

Best regards, Jasper

This reaction accomplishes two things:

1. It shows that I take full responsibility for John's dissatisfaction

2. It demonstrates that I have taken immediate action to remedy the issues

In short, providing a direct and honest reaction shows that you *care about your guest's experience*. A solid response like this will likely nullify the negative effect of the review, assuming that these reviews are few and far between. In fact, if you play your cards right, you could come out of the situation with a stronger reputation than before.

Cristophe's Story

Living in Chicago has been a dream for my wife and me. The city is bursting with fun activities, and the summers are full of energy and excitement. After working in Chicago for many years, I finally realized that it was time to commit to my beloved city once and for all. So my wife and I purchased a three-bedroom condominium in the heart of downtown.

Owning a condo has been a lot of fun. We have a perfect spot to throw parties and entertain guests, and our day-to-day life is very comfortable. But after residing in the unit for over a year, we realized that we had extra space that simply was not being used. Sure, the extra bedrooms will come in handy when we have kids, but that life event is still a ways down the road.

Since our condo has two floors (and we rarely spend time in the downstairs area), we thought it made perfect sense to rent out the downstairs portion. We weren't interested in committing to a long-term tenant because we wanted the freedom to have our place to ourselves during particular times of the year. Moreover, a roommate would not have generated enough cash to compensate for the burden of having someone around all the time.

Short-term renters, on the other hand, are much easier to manage. They come to your place only to sleep, as they usually spend the daytime and evening sightseeing. So after a brief think, we decided to give Airbnb a try. We thought our apartment would be attractive given the abundance of space, the high-end home theater system, and the terrific location. Long story short, we were right!

Demand for our place was high right from the get-go. But we soon realized that prices needed to be flexible to account for seasonal variation. As you might imagine, the demand in January when temperatures reach -20° F isn't nearly as strong as during the lovely summer months. To adjust for these fluctuations, our prices range from $60 per night in the winter to $170 in the summer. The money we earn covers the mortgage and sometimes provides us with a bit of spending cash. Thanks to Airbnb, we live in a brand new, 2,200 square foot luxury condo in downtown Chicago for free!

Airbnb has impacted our lives in an amazing way. We eat out regularly, go on fancy holidays, and indulge our shopping desires. We are able to live a great life with the peace of mind that the bulk of our bills will be paid off by our condo. In addition, we are now looking to expand our rental business to other apartments in the city. We are thrilled that we came across this wonderful website, and can't wait to see what the future brings!

CHAPTER 6

Promoting Your Listing

*"Creative without strategy is called 'art.'
Creative with strategy is called 'advertising.'"*

- Jef L. Richards, Department Chair
and Professor of Advertising
at Michigan State University

F or guests to make a booking, they must be able to find your listing. Pretty basic truism, right? The key to making your listing accessible is by pumping up its search rank. Airbnb automatically includes all relevant listings in its search results, but precisely where you show up amidst the mix of available apartments is the key factor for your success. There are other ways to promote your listing as well, which we will explore in this section.

Airbnb listing search

Just like any other search engine, Airbnb employs a search algorithm to determine the ranking of its listings. One of your biggest challenges during your Airbnb career is to get your listing to the first page of the search results for your neighborhood or city. Showing up on the first page of the search results will contribute greatly to maximizing the number of inquiries and bookings.

Search ranking factors

Nobody knows precisely how Airbnb calculates the ranking of the search results. Airbnb has, however, disclosed a list of data points that they consider. Here's what Airbnb states on its website:

> *"We often hear from hosts that they want a better understanding of how Airbnb determines the ordering of search results. Search ranking is a complex process that takes into account many factors. Because we take so many factors into account, comparing listings based on just a few characteristics doesn't tell the whole story. We're constantly working on improving search to better match guests and hosts, so the factors we use and how we use them can change over time.*
> *Still, there's an underlying principle that guides our approach to search: we want to reward hosts that deliver a*

great experience to guests. This means that as a host, you have control over many of the factors we'll explain below. The way you list your space and look after your guests can have an impact on where you appear in search compared to other listings. But guest preferences also play an important role in how listings are displayed in search results, so you shouldn't expect your listing to appear the same way in search for every guest on Airbnb."

After reviewing the Airbnb website, reading a number of Airbnb related publications, and relying on my extensive experience, I have extracted the following factors that affect placement in the search rankings. I have divided these factors into two categories: (1) Verified factors and (2) Inferred factors. The former category includes factors that have been openly acknowledged by Airbnb. The latter category lists factors that have not been verified, but are believed to influence search rank.

Verified factors

- **Booking appeal** – Airbnb tends to favor high-quality and accurate listings. If there is a tendency for potential guests to view and book your listing, your search rank will benefit. In order to optimize your search results, Airbnb recommends that you "make the title and description attractive and informative" and "explain what makes your space unique."

- **Price** – You should strive to make your price competitive with comparable listings in your area. The logic behind this is that the more competitively priced your listing, the more likely guests will be to book your home. This translates to greater revenue for Airbnb.

- **Quality/Quantity of ratings and reviews** - The better your overall rating, the better your listing's position. Yes, it's pretty straightforward. With respect to the quality of the written reviews, they are actually quantified. I'm not sure precisely how, but Airbnb has reportedly developed a mechanism by which to quantify the written text. Accordingly, I suggest you aim to get as much positive feedback as possible in the ratings and the written reviews.

- **Photos** – Your photos should be of high quality and accurately reflect your space. You should make sure to include at least one photo of each room that is accessible to the guest. In order to ace this category, I recommend making use of Airbnb's free professional photography service.

- **Trust and verification** – Airbnb offers several ways for members to add levels of trust and verification, such as: (1) connecting your Airbnb account to several social media platforms and (2) verifying your ID and telephone number. Make sure to utilize all of the available options.

- **Responsiveness** – This refers to two factors: (1) Response Rate and (2) Response Time. Both are displayed prominently on your listing. This is what it should look like:

Responding quickly to inquiries and booking requests isn't only important for the search results, but it's a key piece of basic customer service. Moreover, a potential customer is more likely to make an inquiry when your listing demonstrates that you are highly responsive. Many potential guests are looking to make plans in the near future. If they believe they will have to wait a few days to hear from you, they may decide to forgo an inquiry altogether.

- **Updated calendar** – An updated calendar improves a user's experience, so it makes sense that Airbnb takes this into account. Make sure your calendar is updated every day. Visiting your calendar page is sufficient to have Airbnb mark it as updated.

- **Acceptance rate** – Pre-approving and accepting booking requests can improve your search rank. Airbnb looks at your overall acceptance rate of bookings as a factor. If you need to reject an application, it is best to officially "Decline" the reservation. This will have a reduced effect on your search rank versus simply sending a message or not responding at all.

- **Cancellation** – Airbnb has made it clear that the cancellation of reservations is a major faux pas. For guests, having a reservation cancelled is a very negative experience. Accordingly, that action will subject your listing to a drop in the rankings.

- **"Instant Book"** – The "Instant Book" feature enables guests to make an instantaneous booking. It negates the need for host approval. Airbnb has stated that "[t]urning on Instant Book may help you in [the] search because guests won't have to wait for a response or worry about getting rejected."

- **Neighborhood** – When guests search for accommodations by city without specifying a neighborhood, Airbnb will favor certain central and popular areas. If your neighborhood is a favorite of the Airbnb algorithm, you will get the benefit of a search bump.

- **Social connections** – If a guest has friends in common with a host, Airbnb will be more likely to show the connected host more prominently to that particular guest. In order to benefit from social connections, be sure to connect your Airbnb account to your Facebook account.

Inferred factors

- **Number of bookings** – Just like a greater number of ratings and reviews will bump your rank, overall bookings should spike your position as well. If these bookings are accompanied by solid reviews, then all the better; but getting these numbers up alone will likely help you regardless.

- **Wish list** – When looking for a perfect place to stay, users can add a listing to their "Wish List." The number of times your space has been added to a Wish List is displayed on your listing below the blue booking button. Although you can't directly influence this metric, I recommend asking previous guests to add your space to their Wish List.

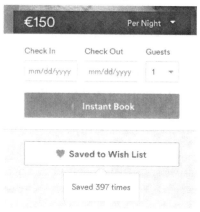

- **Friend recommendations** – Even if you haven't booked a single guest, your friends can set up Airbnb accounts and write recommendations for you and your place. These recommendations will help boost your search rankings, and will also make your listing appear more attractive to potential guests.

- Promoting your listing outside of Airbnb
  If you are just starting out, I recommend running an advertising campaign outside of Airbnb to boost views. I suggest using the following social media tools:
  - Facebook
  - Twitter
  - Personal email to your contacts
  - Sidebar on a personal website or blog
  - Google Adwords

Make every effort to push the bounds on this front, but recognize that all of these methods are merely means to increasing your ranking within Airbnb. At the end of the day, the organic Airbnb rankings are the keys to the castle.

CHAPTER 7

Final Words

"Now this is not the end. It is not even the beginning of the end. But it is, perhaps, the end of the beginning."

**- Winston Churchill,
Former Prime Minister
of the United Kingdom**

Congratulations, you've made it to the end! If you've applied my nuggets of advice, I'm 100% confident that your Airbnb career is off to a good start. Or, if you're already an experienced host, I hope you've found plenty of fresh tips and insights to increase your bookings and overall revenue.

A final word for those who are just starting out on Airbnb: don't delay another day! Every moment you wait is money out of your pocket. Get your listing up and start bringing in the guests.

What is next?

Running a successful Airbnb listing isn't easy. Questions will invariably arise that are tricky to answer. For folks who are interested in personalized and tailored interactive support, Please check out my awesome website called Airbnb Academy.

Thank you!

Thank you for your support and time! I hope you enjoyed reading *Get Paid For Your Pad*, and I look forward to hearing about your progress. If you have any extra time, I would love to hear your thoughts. Please shoot me an email at info@getpaidforyourpad.com. I personally read every single email, so don't be too shy to say hello!

About The Authors

Jasper Ribbers is a former arbitrage trader who now travels full time while running a collection of online businesses from his laptop. He is an avid host on Airbnb, and has consulted numerous individuals on their property listings. He shares his life with the world through his blog, The Traveling Dutchman. After receiving his master's degree in econometrics from the University of Groningen, he worked for a trading firm in Amsterdam, Antwerp, and Chicago. When not on the road, Jasper is based in Amsterdam, The Netherlands.

Huzefa Kapadia is an attorney turned entrepreneur and travel aficionado. He is the owner and founder of Scalar Learning LLC, an education services company that focuses on math tutoring and standardized test preparation. He received his B.S. in computer science and B.A. in economics from the University of Michigan, and earned his J.D. at Northwestern University. He was a patent litigator for four years, specializing in software and hardware related technologies. He now splits his time between his budding business, his various writing projects, and world travel. He lives in Los Angeles, California.

CPSIA information can be obtained at www.ICGtesting.com
Printed in the USA
LVOW10s1455230415

435824LV00019B/648/P